This book is dedicated to all who find Nature not an adversary to conquer and destroy, but a storehouse of infinite knowledge and experience linking man to all things past and present. They know conserving the natural environment is essential to our future well-being.

YELLOWSTONE'S GEYSERS

THE STORY BEHIND THE SCENERY®

by Duncan Foley

DUNCAN FOLEY has taught courses for the Yellowstone Association Institute for more than 25 years with an emphasis on Yellowstone's volcano and its geysers, hot springs, mud pots and fumaroles. He teaches in the Department of Geosciences at Pacific Lutheran University in Tacoma, Washington.

Yellowstone National Park, *located in the northwestern corner of Wyoming, is the world's first national park. Established in 1872, it preserves unparalleled geothermal features.*

Front cover: White Dome Geyser, Lower Geyser Basin; photo by Laurence Parent. Inside Front Cover: Aerial view of Grand Prismatic Hot Spring, Midway Geyser Basin; photo by Duncan Foley. Page 1: Sawmill Geyser, Upper Geyser Basin, photo by Salvatore Vasapolli. Pages 2-3: Old Faithful Geyser from Geyser Hill; photo by Salvatore Vasapolli.

Edited by Maryellen Conner • Book design by K. C. DenDooven.

YELLOWSTONE'S GEYSERS: THE STORY BEHIND THE SCENERY © 2006 KC PUBLICATIONS, INC.
"The Story Behind the Scenery"; the Eagle / Flag icon on Front Cover are registered in the U.S. Patent and Trademark Office.
LC 2006920235. ISBN 0-88714-264-8.

T"The Park is a region of wonder, terror and delight. Nature puts
forth all her powers, and her moods are ever changing from
"grave to gay, from lively to severe." Here tremendous geysers shoot
up their mighty fountains, causing the earth to groan and tremble . . .

. . . by their violence; countless hot springs, indescribable in their strange beauty, show depths as translucent as the ambient air; pools of seething mud, casting up jets of colored paste, bewildered by their curious activity." -Henry J. Winser, 1883

Yellowstone's Geysers
and—
It's a Hydrothermal Story Too!

DUNCAN FOLEY

When fur trappers in the early 1800s told tales of water rushing up from the earth, they were not believed. Today Yellowstone's geysers attract tourists from all over the world. Indeed, the existence of geysers is one of the primary reasons that this area was originally set aside as the first national park.

Yellowstone is the world's greatest concentration of geysers. It is so amazing that if the only geysers were the ones on Geyser Hill in the Upper Geyser Basin, which is about the size of 20 football fields, it would still be a world famous destination for geysers. All the rest of the geysers in the park are just like icing on a cake; they add great fun and wonder to an already fantastic experience.

But why is Yellowstone home to more than one-half of the world's geysers? It takes heat, water, fractures and preservation for geysers to exist. Almost all geysers in the world are found in volcanic areas where very hot rocks provide great heat. Silica from volcanic rocks lines the unique fractures and channels through which geysers erupt. The high mountains also have had plentiful rain and snow in the geologic past, which provides the water that now erupts from the geysers. The area's many earthquakes keep subterranean plumbing open. And hydrothermal systems in the National Park have been preserved in their natural state, rather than being developed. All these factors combine to create and preserve geysers in Yellowstone.

The power of geysers is amazing. Massive jets of heated water, driven by the physical expansion of water into steam, rise far above the land surface. Some geysers shoot their water straight up and some, like Daisy Geyser in the Upper Geyser Basin, shoot their water at an angle.

Minerva Terrace at Mammoth Hot Springs displays characteristic small steps, or terraces, that form in this area. Water flows slowly through pools, and where it spills over the edges, travertine rims can form. These terraces are brightly colored by microbes where hot waters flow. Where dry, and no heat loving microbes live, the terraces are gray to white in color.

Why are some features called geysers and some called hot springs? Geysers intermittently erupt hot water and steam. Hot springs flow without an eruption. In Yellowstone, once a feature has erupted as a geyser, it often continues to be called a geyser, even if it hasn't erupted for a long time. For example, Excelsior Geyser in Midway Geyser Basin erupted in the 1880s, and then didn't erupt again until briefly in the mid-1980s. Although it now primarily acts as just a huge hot spring, occasional boils to several feet suggest that it may erupt again in the future. Therefore Excelsior is called a geyser, not a hot spring.

Geysers such as Old Faithful are different from hot springs in that they have an unusual characteristic in their plumbing systems: there are narrow spots in subsurface geyser channels that allow pressures and temperatures to build up below the constrictions.

Geysers, despite the awesome force of their eruptions, also have a delicate balance of the rates of recharge of heat and water to their systems. If there is too little or too much water, or too little or too much heat, the geyser will not erupt.

Massive geyser eruptions can be awe inspiring, but there are also rewards in looking at small features. These lily-pad like sinter formations are a form of silica that is deposited from hot spring waters, typically where silica-rich volcanic rocks are located underground.

*Geysers will have one of two
long term fates...
Some geysers last for centuries
and others may erupt only rarely.*

A Geyser Eruption

Two physical facts must be kept in mind to understand an eruption of a geyser:

1. Water boils at a higher temperature when it is under higher pressure and lower temperature when it is under lower pressure, and

2. When liquid water converts to steam (boils), its volume expands by more than 1500 times.

The first point is critical, and fortunately easy to understand. At sea level, where atmospheric pressure is higher, water boils at 212°F (100°C). At the elevation of Yellowstone, where atmospheric pressure is lower, water boils at a about 199°F (93°C).

Increase pressure and the boiling point temperature rises. The lid on a kitchen pressure cooker raises the boiling temperature of water (and therefore cooks food faster) by increasing pressure on the water.

The second point is fundamental science. When a substance (in this case water) changes from a liquid to gas, the volume it can fill expands.

As a geyser begins to recharge, it needs both water and heat. The underground water comes through cracks and fractures in subterranean rocks. The heat to warm the water comes from rocks that are next to the cracks and fractures. If a geyser has a visible pool, water levels easily can be observed to rise as recharge occurs.

In some geyser systems there are underground cavities that can store water for the next eruption. At Old Faithful there is at least one underground cavity that is more than 6 feet (1.8m) in diameter at a depth of approximately 35 to 40 feet (11-13m) below the rim.

DUNCAN FOLEY

Vapor rises from Old Faithful's vent between eruptions. Small pools near the vent are not visible from the boardwalk. The mounds at the side of the vent are reported to be tree stumps encrusted by deposits from the geyser water.

SALVATORE VASAPOLLI

If visitors see only one geyser, it is almost certain to be Old Faithful. The vent is at the northwest side of a long mound, which can be seen rising above the people in the photograph. Much of the mound may be from older hot spring activity that predates the geyser eruptions of Old Faithful.

Will Cistern someday Steal *Energy* from Steamboat?

In the subterranean plumbing of a geyser before it erupts, slightly cooler water lies above the deeper, hotter water that is starting to boil. This cooler water acts as a lid and increases pressure and, therefore, the temperature of the water below. As deeper water starts to boil, bubbles form. These bubbles rise into the overlying cooler water and condense. The rising bubbles also carry heat from depth up to warm the overlying water.

Geyser plumbing systems often have a near-surface constriction. In Old Faithful, the constriction is slightly larger than 4 inches (11 cm) across at a depth of 22 ft (6.8 m). As pre-eruption bubbles form, some of the larger bubbles and uprising water may not be able to pass thorough the constriction, and become trapped. This trapping increases pressures and water temperatures below even more.

Eventually the force of uprising water will push bubbles through the constriction and all the way to the water's surface. If all the water in the geyser vent is hot enough when forceful bubbles break the water surface, the pressure below is lowered, and the waters below boil quickly (flash) to steam. The conversion of liquid water to steam provides the energy to push geyser waters to great heights.

In some geysers, such as Old Faithful, rather than the calm process described above, pre-eruption water violently boils and surges in the geyser column. This violent boiling eventually rises to the land

Cliff Geyser in Black Sand Basin erupts from a vent that sits within just a few feet of Iron Springs Creek. It is named for the wall of geyser deposits that separates the geyser and its pool from the river. Cliff Geyser illustrates how a deep hot water system, which is represented at the surface by geysers and other hydrothermal features, is largely separate from colder surface waters, represented by the river.

DUNCAN FOLEY

Grand Geyser (on the right), Turban Geyser (in the center) and Vent Geyser (on the left) illustrate how three geysers can share one plumbing system. Grand will often be triggered to erupt during an eruption of Turban, and Vent usually starts after both Grand and Turban are going. Of these three, Grand rises the highest, occasionally reaching close to 200 feet. Be sure to check Park Service predictions for eruptions of Grand Geyser, as typical eruptions last longer than Old Faithful, and many observers feel that Grand is much more spectacular than Old Faithful.

DUNCAN FOLEY

surface, where it can be seen as pre-eruption splashes (and heard in the clicking of cameras).

Once the water and steam in the underground plumbing system have emptied, the geyser eruption will end. Often the final phase of a geyser eruption is steam, without liquid water. The steam is formed from the last water in the underground fractures. In pool-type geysers, such as Grand Geyser in the Upper Geyser Basin or Echinus Geyser in the Norris Geyser Basin, it is easy to see that the pool is much lower (or even gone) at the end of the eruption.

Of course there are many variations in the basic process of how geysers erupt. Some geysers erupt from pools and some from cones. Some geysers, such as Grand, Turban and Vent in the Upper Geyser Basin, share plumbing systems. Some geysers, such as Daisy in the Upper Geyser Basin, may cool off when wind is blowing hard, and the interval between eruptions can lengthen.

Geysers typically will have one of two long-term fates; they will deposit minerals in their channels and seal themselves off, or they will blow themselves apart. Some geysers last for centuries and others may erupt only rarely.

If a geyser chokes itself off with minerals, its subterranean water can be diverted along other

Scientists, using water chemistry, can tell that Norris Geyser Basin has some of the hottest underground waters of all the geyser basins in Yellowstone. The geysers, fumaroles and hot springs at Norris are quite often prone to change their activity from one type to another.

In September 1989, Porkchop Geyser in the Back Basin at Norris Geyser Basin blew itself apart. Fragments of the geyser deposits now lie jumbled around the pool that formed after the eruption. One block included a portion of the vent, which can be seen lined with minerals. A boardwalk takes visitors near the pool.

underground fractures, and nearby thermal features may change. If the channels only partially plugged, however, and there are not alternative routes for waters to follow, higher pressure can build up underground and the geyser can erupt and destroy its plumbing system. Porkchop Geyser, in the back basin at Norris, had just such an eruption, which is called a hydrothermal explosion, in 1989. Porkchop Geyser became a quiet spring; however, silica minerals deposited in its channels may rebuild and restore its plumbing, and it could erupt again.

Geysers may also die by having their water or heat "stolen" by another geyser. Sometimes waters that flowed to one geyser will instead flow along subterranean fractures to another, and the first will cease to erupt. Such connections may be easy or difficult to establish. At Norris Geyser Basin, Cistern Spring (not a geyser) drains after every eruption of Steamboat Geyser. Will Cistern someday steal the energy from Steamboat?

Yellowstone's hydrothermal systems are dynamic. Changes in temperatures, flow rates, or durations of eruptions and intervals between eruptions of geysers are typical; it is unusual for hydrothermal systems to remain the same for many seasons. We can expect that what we see today will change tomorrow.

Nature's kitchen requires the right combinations of ingredients - heat, water and fractured rocks - to make geysers, hot springs, mud pots and fumaroles. Alter heat by cooling or heating the magma, change water by reducing or increasing thermal subterranean flow or by changing the amount of boiling or mixing with cooler, near-surface groundwater, or modify fractures by sealing with minerals or opening by earthquake shaking, and the hydrothermal systems and their surface features will change. It is indeed amazing, given the fragility of the systems and the dynamic nature of the earth, that so many geysers have been so regular for more than a century. Many geysers may only be an earthquake away from permanent changes.

FRED HIRSCHMANN

Eruptions of Steamboat, the world's tallest active geyser, are relatively rare. Intervals between eruptions have ranged from days to decades. Steamboat is named for the tremendous noise that it makes while erupting. A typical eruption consists of only a few minutes of water, which can reach 300 feet high, followed by 12 hours or more of steam.

- 11 -

Legend:

- water seepage from rain and snow
- heated water forced up through the rocks
- heated water that has turned into steam
- Limestone
- Tuff and breccia
- Lava flow
- Shale
- Caldera Lava flow
- Sandstone

HEAT

HEAT

HEAT

Where deep-circulating waters encounter buried limestone, the limestone may dissolve. As these waters flow upward, they lose their ability to hold the dissolved limestone, which is deposited at the surface as a rock called travertine. This is the kind of rock that is forming at Mammoth Hot Springs.
(p. 32-35)

Waters that eventually rise as geysers, hot springs, mud pots and fumaroles originally fell as rain or snow on the high mountains around Yellowstone. These waters then seep underground, where they move through fractures and along faults. As the waters flow underground, they dissolve elements from the rocks they flow through, and they pick up heat from deep magma.
(p. 20-23)

Roaring Mountain is an example of a hydrothermal system where steam rather than liquid water is the dominant form of fluid that is rising from depth. The steam forms fumaroles (gas vents) and/ or mud pots when it reaches the surface. Vapor areas are typically very acidic and often smell of hydrogen sulfide gas.
(p. 24-25; 28-29)

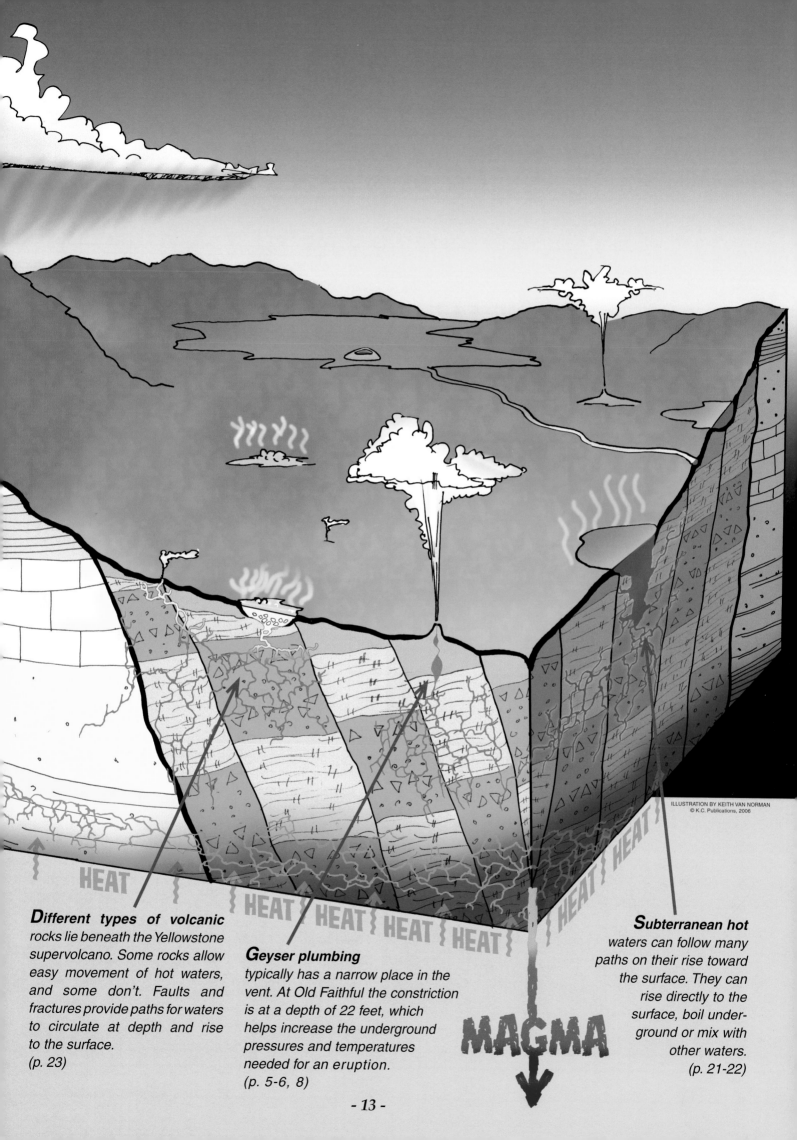

ILLUSTRATION BY KEITH VAN NORMAN
© K.C. Publications, 2006

HEAT

HEAT ⟩ HEAT ⟩ HEAT ⟩ HEAT ⟩

HEAT ⟩ HEAT ⟩

Different types of volcanic rocks lie beneath the Yellowstone supervolcano. Some rocks allow easy movement of hot waters, and some don't. Faults and fractures provide paths for waters to circulate at depth and rise to the surface.
(p. 23)

Geyser plumbing typically has a narrow place in the vent. At Old Faithful the constriction is at a depth of 22 feet, which helps increase the underground pressures and temperatures needed for an eruption.
(p. 5-6, 8)

MAGMA

Subterranean hot waters can follow many paths on their rise toward the surface. They can rise directly to the surface, boil underground or mix with other waters.
(p. 21-22)

*Geologic detectives have brought us
our current level of awareness;
future studies will help reveal the more
fascinating aspects of this great story.*

A Land of Water and Heat

FRED HIRSCHMANN

Yellowstone National Park has the world's greatest concentration of geysers, hot springs, mudpots and fumaroles. Collectively, these are known as hydrothermal, or natural hot water, systems. Why are there so many here? Yellowstone has the exceptional combination of a young volcano, lots of precipitation, and many earthquakes to keep deep rock fractures open. Individual hydrothermal sites are created by the dynamic geological interaction of water, heat, and rock.

GEOLOGISTS ARE DETECTIVES OF DEEP TIME AND FAR UNDERGROUND

Geologists are detectives of Earth's history and its natural processes. They look at features, such as Yellowstone's hydrothermal systems, and ask questions. Why are so many amazing geysers, hot springs, mud pots and fumaroles located here? Why is Yellowstone unique in the world? How do the hydrothermal features form? What is it about the history and plumbing of a geyser that makes it different from a hot spring or a mud pot? Why are these

The smaller hot spring in the foreground *reflects the boiling heat of the thermal pool behind it. In many hot spring areas white zones often indicate areas too hot for colorful microbes to live, although some Yellowstone microbes can survive in boiling water. As waters flow away from hot spring vents and cool, brightly-colored microbes can begin to live.*

DUNCAN FOLEY

Beehive Geyser erupts
*from a remarkable cone
that is built on a broad shield of
older hot spring and geyser deposits.
Watch for a small geyser erupting
a few feet high near the main cone.
It may indicate that a spectacular eruption
of Beehive is just a few minutes away.*

systems so changeable on human and geologic time scales? What microscopic forms of life live in these waters? How does life itself survive at such temperatures? What does the future hold?

Detectives use on-site and laboratory evidence as pieces of a puzzle to try to figure out how an event occurred. Geologists use evidence from both field observations of hydrothermal systems and laboratory study of their waters and deposits to understand how geologic features have developed and changed over time. Geological evidence ranges from microscopic, such as studies of geyser deposits, to continental, such as how the Yellowstone volcano fits into the history of North America.

Geologists extend their vision through space and time. They are interested in subsurface processes, in addition to what can be seen at the surface. They recognize that what is seen today is just a snapshot in time. Before today there were ancient seas, long-extinct volcanoes and grinding glaciers thousands of feet thick. After today there will be yet untold changes in what we now see.

For geologists, a description of a physical feature such as a spring is foremost among field evidence. What is its temperature? How acid is it? What are the colors of life forms growing in the water?

This small hot spring in the Lower Geyser Basin is perched on a deposit of sinter (silica from hot springs and geysers). In order for sinter to be deposited when thermal waters reach the surface, underground temperatures must be at least 180 degrees C. It is typical for hot springs and geysers to flow from low areas near rivers. The Firehole River flows in the background.

FRED HIRSCHMANN

Does it erupt? Does it flow? Is there mud? Are there gasses? Often geologists, with appropriate National Park Service research permits, will gather small samples of waters, spring deposits, gasses or muds to take back to the laboratory to study in more detail.

Geologic evidence from rocks and waters, gathered in both field and laboratory, is used to interpret the story of each hydrothermal feature. The history is understood, the present is interpreted, and the future is suggested on the basis of geological processes and products. Geologic detectives have brought us to our current level of awareness; future studies will help reveal more fascinating aspects of this great story.

A Dynamic Geologic Recipe

Four key ingredients are required to create the hydrothermal systems seen today. These are water, heat, fractured rock and preservation. The word "hydrothermal" combines both "hydro," indicating a major role for water and/or steam, and "thermal," indicating a major role for earth's heat. Water comes from the hydrologic system and heat comes from magma and hot rocks in the Yellowstone volcano and its deep roots. The right kinds of rocks and fractures are needed to allow waters that have been

heated at depth to be able to rise to the surface. And, for much longer than a century, these marvels of nature have been preserved in a National Park.

Yellowstone – a Hot Volcano

Yellowstone, a park of many superlatives, easily takes the title of the largest geologically young volcano in the United States. But why is Yellowstone considered a supervolcano, and why is it located here? What does being such a large volcano have to do with the geysers, hot springs, mud pots and fumaroles? Other large volcanoes of the same approximate age exist around the world, but only Yellowstone has such a unique concentration of hydrothermal systems.

About 640,000 years ago, the youngest of a long series of immense volcanoes erupted in the area now known as Yellowstone National Park. About 240 cubic miles (1000 cubic kilometers) of new rock (about 1000 times larger than the 1980 eruption of Mount St. Helens) were produced during this eruption. This volume of new material is equivalent to a cube slightly larger than six miles long, six miles wide and six miles high. A caldera, or volcanic collapse crater, more than 25 by 50 miles across, formed as a result of the eruption. The area of the caldera is about the size of the state of Rhode Island. Even today,

JOHN P. GEORGE

Gibbon Falls and the Gibbon River are near the edge of the 640,000-year-old caldera of the Yellowstone supervolcano. The margins of the caldera are difficult to see because the down dropped part of the volcano has been filled with younger volcanic rocks.

What lies beneath geyser basins? Fractures that cut volcanic rocks, such as these in the walls of the Grand Canyon of the Yellowstone, can serve as pathways for hot waters.

after more than 600 millennia of erosion, deposits of ash from this enormous eruption are still found as far away as California and Texas.

For at least the last 16 million years, the western United States has been the scene of huge volcanic eruptions. One chain of massive, caldera-forming volcanoes marks the current track of the Snake River Plain in Idaho. Many geologists interpret this chain of volcanoes as the product of the North American continent moving over a hot spot, which is an unusual concentration of heat that rises from beneath the earth's crust.

Around the globe there are many hot spots that make volcanoes. The Hawaiian Islands formed as a chain of volcanoes as the Pacific plate of Earth's crust drifted over a hot spot. At Yellowstone, hot spot heat melts overlying continental crust, which then can form silica-rich volcanic rocks known as rhyolites and tuffs. The silica, dissolved from the rocks by hot waters, is an important component in the development of hydrothermal systems at Yellowstone.

The Yellowstone eruption of 640,000 years ago was the youngest of three major volcanic eruption sequences in this area. The oldest eruption sequence took place about 2.1 million years ago, and the middle took place about 1.3 million years ago. The three eruption sequences overlapped in area, with the

The balance of the amount of heat and the amount of water determines what kinds of thermal features form at the surface. In areas where there is lots of subsurface heat and boiling is taking place underground, steam flows through fractures to create fumaroles such as this one in Norris Geyser Basin.

Chocolate Pots are located near the main highway west of Norris Geyser Basin. The distinctive reddish-brown colors of these pots are due to iron-fixing microbes. These microbes may be related to some of the earliest microbes on earth, which may have contributed to the formation of iron ore deposits over a billion years ago.

oldest eruption being the largest, the middle nestling in the western side of the first, and the youngest overlapping and extending east of the first.

Eruptions at Yellowstone have stacked three tiers of volcanic rocks upon each other, much as a baker may stack layer cakes upon layer cakes to build a tiered wedding cake. Each individual tier of the cake may be built from a bottom layer of cake, a layer of filling, and a top layer of cake. The final cake is then put together, building a stack of individually layered tiers.

At Yellowstone, rhyolites are the first-erupted rocks, and thus oldest and bottom rocks in each three-part tier. Rhyolites usually erupt as thick, sticky lavas. When cooled, they fracture easily and therefore form the aquifers, or underground water-bearing layers, for Yellowstone's tiered hydrothermal systems.

But what is below ALL these Volcanic Rocks?

Vapor rises from appropriately named Circle Pool in the Midway Geyser Basin. Flood Geyser erupts to the left of Circle Pool, and many other vents can be seen in the cool evening light.

The middle layer of each volcanic tier is formed from massive eruptions called pyroclastic flows. These are huge ash clouds that blanket the countryside many tens of feet deep in hot (1100°F; 600°C), fast moving (more than 100 miles per hour; 160 km per hour) blasts of ash and gas. Rocks that form from pyroclastic flows are known as tuffs, which do not fracture as easily as rhyolites. Therefore tuffs form layers that typically are not good hydrothermal aquifers.

Large pyroclastic eruptions can remove much of the magma from an underground magma chamber. Once the chamber is at least partially emptied, the ground above it collapses to form a caldera.

The top layer of each volcanic tier is formed from more rhyolites. This layer is stacked on the first layer of rhyolites and the middle layer of tuffs. This youngest layer of rhyolites can fill the caldera left after the eruption of the tuff. The 640,000 year old Yellowstone caldera has been filled by such rhyolites.

A *small bubble bursts the surface of this hot spring in* Norris Geyser Basin. Some rising bubbles in hot springs can cool, condense and implode before they reach the surface.

FRED HIRSCHMANN

Not everything that erupts is large. This small hot spring at Norris splashes water next to itself, where it has built intricate sinter deposits. In a hot splash zone such as surrounds this spring, the yellow colors are likely mineral deposits.

SALVATORE VASAPOLLI

This is why visitors do not see a large collapsed crater when they visit the park.

Although most volcanic rocks erupt from within and on the edge of the caldera, some eruptions also can occur outside the caldera. These eruptions can be either rhyolite or basalt, which is a relatively silica-poor and very fluid volcanic rock.

The repetition of caldera-forming volcanic tiers means that below the surface rocks, there is a stacked sequence of rhyolites and tuffs, some of which allow subterranean hot waters to flow easily, and some of which restrict flow.

But what is below all these volcanic rocks? There probably are older rocks that existed before the volcanism started, and rocks from magma that never erupted but instead cooled well below the land surface. Volcanoes only destroy pre-existing rocks in the actual vents of the eruptions, which at Yellowstone were located in two narrow rings.

If Yellowstone were viewed from directly above during the eruption, the rings of vents would overlap much like two of the rings of the Olympic symbol. In drawings of the Olympic rings, there typically is a background color that is both inside and outside of the rings. This background color can be visualized as similar to the pre-volcanic rocks of Yellowstone. These pre-existing rocks, with their faults and fractures, remain both inside and outside the rings of vents.

In many places now cooled and solid magma lies below the remnants of the pre-existing rocks. One distinctive aspect of Yellowstone, however, is that geologists think that there still is magma, or molten rock, active beneath Yellowstone. This magma provides heat for the hydrothermal systems, and changes in the magma can help keep Yellowstone geologically dynamic.

RAIN AND SNOW FROM THE PAST

The volcano provides rocks and heat. Rain and melted snow, sinking deep underground, provide the water.

PAT O'HARA

Riverside Geyser erupts over the Firehole River. Riverside has erupted approximately every six to six and a half hours for many years. Why some geysers erupt in a very regular pattern and others don't may be related to how few or how many subterranean connections exist between different hydrothermal features.

The continuous circulation of water in the hydrologic system is also known as the water cycle. In the hydrologic system, water in the ocean evaporates to the atmosphere and is brought over land by atmospheric circulation. Once over land, the atmospheric water falls as rain or snow. The water that lands on the ground can be used by plants, run off into rivers and lakes, or soak into the ground to become groundwater. Water that circulates to great depths can become heated by hot rocks and rise to form geysers, hot springs, mud pots and fumaroles.

Ultimately, many of the hydrothermal systems may be connected at depth, but different waters rise along different flow paths, encounter different rocks and different temperatures, and develop different chemistries. The distinctive subterranean fates of the waters create the great variety of hydrothermal features we see at the surface.

To understand Yellowstone's hydrothermal systems, it is important to appreciate that groundwater moves slowly. Whereas river waters may flow several miles per hour, groundwater beneath Yellowstone may flow at rates of about a mile per decade to a mile per century.

How old are the waters that erupt from Yellowstone's geysers? Using indirect methods, geologists estimate that the waters we see erupting today fell as rain or snow, perhaps 150 to 1500 years ago. What is known is that the climate in which the geyser waters fell as precipitation was cooler than the present climate on the Yellowstone plateau.

From about 150 to about 550 years ago there was a "little ice age," and the climate at Yellowstone was much cooler than it is now. Cooler climates can also be found in the high elevations of the Gallatin Mountains, in the northwest part of the park. The waters that erupt from the geysers and hot springs may, therefore, either be older waters from the little ice age or cooler water from higher in the Gallatin Mountains. Or both.

Note that the caldera-forming eruption sequences built a series of stacked aquifers. Deeper

DUNCAN FOLEY

There is magic in mud pots. Fantastic patterns.
*Gurgles, hisses, pops and splats. Explosions of
mud fly from bursting bubbles. But be sure to
stand clear, as the mud is very hot and very acidic.*

FRED HIRSCHMANN

This small geyser is one of a very few geysers in
*Yellowstone to have acidic water. Most geysers, such as
Old Faithful, have waters that are described by geochemists as
chemically neutral or alkaline. Acidic conditions are common,
however, in areas with mud pots or fumaroles. Echinus Geyser,
in Norris Geyser Basin, is another acidic geyser. Some researchers
suggest that the spiny form of silica deposits, such as seen in the
foreground of this photograph, is more common in acidic waters.*

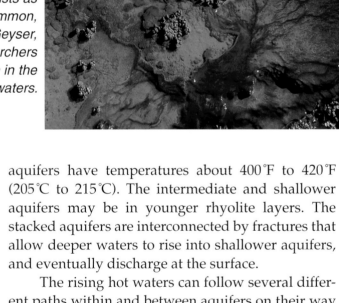

aquifers, those closer to the magma, are going to be hotter. Shallower aquifers are going to be relatively cooler. But how do geologists know how hot waters are at depth?

Geologists look for clues to subsurface temperatures in the chemistry of thermal waters. Deep waters acquire some of their elements from the rocks they flow through; the exact mix of elements can be interpreted to indicate subsurface temperatures. The deepest Yellowstone aquifers have temperatures up to 650°F to 800°F (350°C to 425°C). These deep aquifers are probably located in the oldest rhyolites from the first volcanic sequence, and may be present beneath large sections of the youngest caldera.

Intermediate and shallower aquifers overlie the deepest aquifer. The intermediate aquifer has temperatures slightly above 500°F (270°C). Shallower

aquifers have temperatures about 400°F to 420°F (205°C to 215°C). The intermediate and shallower aquifers may be in younger rhyolite layers. The stacked aquifers are interconnected by fractures that allow deeper waters to rise into shallower aquifers, and eventually discharge at the surface.

The rising hot waters can follow several different paths within and between aquifers on their way up to the surface. Some waters may rise from depth without boiling. Some waters may rise from depth and partially boil. Some waters may completely boil, leaving only steam coming to the surface. And some waters may rise from depth, boil or not boil, and then mix with shallower, cooler groundwater. The multitude of options for hot waters to experience leads ultimately to the wide variety of geysers, hot springs, mud pots and fumaroles in Yellowstone.

Brightly colored microbial mats rim Grand Prismatic Hot Spring and line its outflow channels. Note the blue color of the deep, hot pool, where neither bacteria nor algae grow. As water flows away from the spring and cools, more microbes can survive, and yellows and reds dominate. For an aerial view of this hot spring see the inside front cover.

JOHN P. GEORGE

UNDERGROUND WATER FLOWS THROUGH FRACTURES

The volcano provides rocks and heat, and the hydrologic cycle provides the water. The geologic trick is to move hot water through solid rock quickly enough so the water remains hot on its journey up to the surface. Geologic processes, such as the common earthquakes at Yellowstone, can create open fractures in the volcanic rocks. Where open fractures are interconnected, hydrothermal waters may rise to the surface.

Yellowstone is earthquake country. Many hundreds to thousands of small earthquakes occur each year in and near the park. Sometimes there are large earthquakes, such as the 1959 magnitude 7.5 earthquake just west of the park at Hebgen Lake. The 1959 earthquake was followed by changes in the behavior of geysers and the formation of new geysers. Seismic Geyser, for instance, began to erupt after the earthquake. Even Old Faithful has changed its eruptive pattern after earthquakes, as perhaps some fractures were opened and others were closed.

In volcanic rocks, fractures may be only a few millimeters to centimeters across; they should not be imagined as open caves and flowing rivers. Typical fractures in volcanic rocks can easily be seen in the walls of the Grand Canyon of the Yellowstone and in many road cuts throughout the park.

As hot waters rise through fractures, they may boil, cool, or mix with shallow, cooler waters. Where minerals deposited from hot waters seal fractures, rising hot waters can be seen next to cold waters. Fishing Cone at West Thumb and geysers along the Firehole River illustrates this phenomenon.

Outside the caldera, however, where limestone and other non-volcanic rocks may be located at depth, there probably are places where interconnected cave-like features have thermal groundwater flowing through them. Mammoth is one site where subterranean caves likely exist nearby. All the travertine we see at the surface is chemically similar to limestone and likely was dissolved from limestone that exists in the subsurface.

Overleaf: Early on a cool day, sunlight shines through fumaroles at Roaring Mountain, between Norris and Mammoth. Hydrothermal alteration, or chemical changes brought about by hot acidic steam, has turned the originally dark rocks gray. This area once was much louder; perhaps in the future it will one day roar again. Photo by John P. George.

SANDRA NYKERK

When insects fall into pools, such as this one at Mammoth Hot Springs, they can become chemically coated with travertine or, in many hot spring or geysers areas, sinter. The mineral coverings can preserve many of the fine details of the body and wings of the insects.

Geologists have identified many faults (surfaces along which the rocks have moved relative to each other) in pre-volcanic rocks surrounding the Yellowstone caldera. When the volcano erupted and collapsed, the pre-volcanic rocks and their faults also collapsed and are now buried under younger volcanic rocks. Faults in the pre-volcanic rocks, where they remain fractured and open, are especially likely locations for very deep and hot circulation of groundwater.

Shallow subterranean fractures may also connect surface features. Careful observations of geyser behavior patterns have lead many people to conclude that connections likely exist between selected features. One case of certain connection exists between Steamboat Geyser and Cistern Spring at Norris Geyser Basin. When Steamboat erupts, Cistern, which is located just downhill from the geyser, drains. It can take several days for Cistern to refill after an eruption of its neighbor.

While earthquakes can open fractures in rocks, it is important to note that geological processes also can close the fractures. Hot waters circulating below the caldera can dissolve silica from rocks at depth. When silica-laden hot waters rise and cool along fractures, minerals can form and choke the hydrothermal pathways. The hot waters then must find another channel along which to rise, and existing hot springs or geysers can die and new features can be created.

HYDROTHERMAL SYSTEMS

Hydrothermal systems in Yellowstone can be classified into two general groups based on whether water or steam is rising through subsurface fractures. The first group, with liquid water rising from depth, can be subdivided into two types depending on whether the hot springs deposit silica or travertine. Geysers are located only in silica depositing hot water systems; they are not found in travertine depositing systems. The second group, where steam rather than liquid water is rising, includes mud pots and fumaroles.

DUNCAN FOLEY

Geyserite and hot spring deposits can take many intricate forms. Different textures may result from a variety of factors, including whether an area near a geyser gets splashed during an eruption, whether an area has a pool or constant flowing water, how hot or acidic the water is, and what kinds of microbes live in the waters.

HOT WATER SYSTEMS

If hydrothermal waters journey below the caldera, where they encounter high subsurface temperatures and rocks rich in silica, hot springs and geysers can form that have silica rich surface deposits called "sinter." The typical white to gray rocks characteristic of areas around geysers, such as in the Upper, Midway, Lower and Norris Geyser Basins are sinter. Where sinter has been deposited from a geyser it is called "geyserite."

Geologists studying the chemistry of silica have discovered that it takes subsurface temperatures of about 350°F (180°C) for waters to dissolve enough silica from underground rocks so that sinter deposits will form when the waters reach the surface and cool. So everywhere you see sinter or geysers, very hot waters, well above surface boiling temperatures, are filling rock fractures that are perhaps only a few tens to hundreds of feet below you. Surface temperatures of hot springs and geysers in these areas can be up to the boiling point at the elevation of the springs. This is approximately 199°F (or 93°C) in Yellowstone.

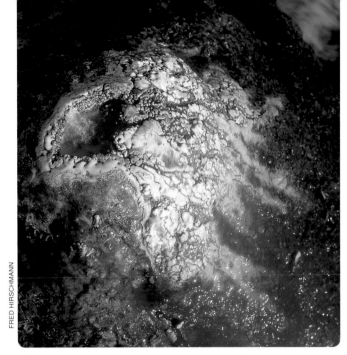

FRED HIRSCHMANN

This small hot spring at the bottom of the *Grand Canyon of the Yellowstone shows vibrant colors from different types of microbes.*

Colors in Morning Glory Pool have become *muted over the years as tourists have thrown debris into it and choked off its water supply. Throwing items, even coins, into pools can plug their plumbing and cool them forever.*

ED COOPER

Canary Spring flows
from the east side of
the terraces at Mammoth. Bubbling at Mammoth is
caused by carbon dioxide coming out of the
waters, not by boiling. There are no places
at Mammoth where the water is hot enough
to boil, so Mammoth has no geysers.

If hydrothermal waters have journeyed in areas where subsurface temperatures are slightly cooler and where underground rocks are rich in limestone, calcium carbonate dissolved from the limestone by the waters can form deposits of a rock called travertine when the waters reach the land surface. Travertine terraces are most prominent at Mammoth Hot Springs, which is located about 18 miles north of the caldera. There are extensive limestone layers in and below the mountains near Mammoth. Because the waters are cooler (well below boiling at the surface), and there is no appropriate geological plumbing system, there are no geysers at Mammoth.

Steam Systems

Some hydrothermal systems in Yellowstone have subsurface geology that is similar to a pot of water boiling on a stove. When water in a pot boils, some of the water changes to steam and rises. If there is a lid on the pot, the steam cools and condenses on the lid (this is the water that runs down your hand and arm when you remove the pan lid to check the spaghetti sauce). If there are chemicals in the boiling water, some rise into the air (and you smell the food) and some, if the pot boils dry, will be left as a crust of salt on the inside of the pot.

Where waters from Mammoth lie in still
pools, a thin layer of calcite can form.
Known informally as "calcite ice," these
layers can take many fascinating shapes.

Steam-rich hydrothermal systems (called "vapor-dominated" because hot water vapor, more than liquid water, is rising) work in a way that is similar to a boiling pot on a stove. Earth's heat (cooling magma under Yellowstone) boils underground waters. The steam rising from underground boiling cools as it reaches the land surface. It condenses like the waters on the pot lid and can make pools at the surface. These pools can also contain local groundwater, rainwater and melted snow. The steam is also carrying some chemical elements and other gasses with it. Like the pot forms a crust of salt, underground boiling leaves some elements behind in the

FRED HIRSCHMANN

An unusual round spring flows from the terraces at Mammoth. The white feather-like streamers in the waters are microbes, along which travertine is precipitating.

WHY right *Here?*

subsurface. Of course, we cannot see these subsurface elements at Yellowstone, but geologists have found them in other extinct, now cooled, eroded and exposed hydrothermal systems.

Sulphur is among the elements that accompany steam. When the sulphur reaches the surface, some is chemically made into sulphuric acid, which corrodes the rocks. Part of the sulphur is also made into the gas hydrogen sulphide, which gives vapor-dominated areas their typical rotten egg odor. Some people do not enjoy vapor-dominated areas because of their smell.

Some of the bright colors in Yellowstone's hydrothermal systems are the result of minerals, not microbes. The vent of this small fumarole is coated with sulphur crystals that are depositing directly out of the rising gasses, a common feature where there is sulphur underground for the gasses to dissolve.

SALVATORE VASAPOLLI

Water streams from a hot spring into the Ferris Fork of the Bechler River in the southwest corner of the park, one of many backcountry areas that have exciting thermal features.

SALVATORE VASAPOLLI

But how deep is the boiling? In some areas, like the multicolored Fountain Paint Pots in the Lower Geyser Basin, the boiling is probably quite shallow. These vents occur at the top of a small hill that is surrounded by geysers. The geysers may represent the level of boiling water; where the hill is only a few feet higher, there is only steam, and a vapor-dominated system forms. In other areas, the boiling water table may be much deeper. A research drill hole demonstrated that boiling water can be more than 100 meters (330 feet) below the land surface.

Typically, vapor-dominated hydrothermal systems have very little water in their runoff channels, as the volume of rising steam is much less than the volume of water that rises in geysers and hot springs. Strong acids attack and convert rocks and soils to gray and black muds and colorful yellow and green deposits.

Fumaroles are hydrothermal gas vents, without a surface pool of condensed water. Some fumaroles become mud pots when there is rain or snow. Some mud pots become fumaroles as they dry out. Grizzly Fumaroles can be wet mud pots in the spring and dry out to gas-only fumaroles during dry summers.

SANDRA NYKERK

A forest of "bobby sox" trees stands around the edge of Opalescent Pool in the Black Sand Geyser Basin. These trees have been killed by hot waters flowing around their base. Their white lower trunks, or "bobby sox," are created as silica from hot spring waters wicks into the wood.

Mud pots can *take many forms. These, in the Lower Geyser Basin, are in the form of a field of mud volcanoes that are one to two feet high. Others are large individual pots, such as this backcountry example, which can throw exploding mud blobs (this mud blob is about five feet across) more than ten feet into the air.*

Why is liquid water rising in some places and steam rising in others? The geologic balance of the recharge of both heat and water contributes to the type of surface feature. Where water recharge is reduced, perhaps because fractures have become plugged, but heat recharge remains high, boiling can take place in the subsurface, and vapor-dominated systems can form.

WHY RIGHT HERE?

Heat, water and fractures make Yellowstone ideal for hydrothermal systems, but why are hot springs and geysers located at their specific sites? Most basins are located, as their name suggests, in low areas where waters can most easily rise. At Old Faithful, for instance, there are hills on the east, south and west sides of the geyser. Vapor systems, however, may be found on hills, where their steam can rise through fractures.

Scientists have discovered that there are likely major fault systems that help water circulate deeply beneath many of the geyser basins. At Norris, for instance, deep faults related to the edge of the caldera are intersected by fracture along a major fault zone that trends north from Norris to Mammoth. There also are lots of earthquakes at Norris, which help keep the fractures open. Small, near-surface faults may help control the locations of many individual hydrothermal features.

An oblong ring of colorful yellow microbes *surrounds a small hydrothermal feature in Biscuit Basin. The debris that covers the microbes near the vent suggests that this feature has had a recent eruption.*

Some myths die hard. The best data suggest that Old Faithful never really had a long-term average of exactly an hour between eruptions.

Places and Happenings

With brilliant white terraces, bubbling springs amid brightly colored channels, and stark trees buried by rock — the vistas that form the hot springs at Mammoth are magnificent indeed. Mammoth Hot Springs are so large and impressive that they were once known as White Mountain.

MAMMOTH

Thermal spring deposits at Mammoth, called travertine, are made of calcium carbonate (not sinter as in geyser basins). Hot, gas-rich waters dissolve limestone layers deep underground. When the waters reach the surface, they lose the gas, which is largely carbon dioxide, in the typical bubbling that is seen at spring vents. The loss of carbon dioxide changes the chemistry of the water, and travertine is deposited.

Once the carbon dioxide has bubbled away at the vents, however, the cooler, gas-poor waters can chemically dissolve the travertine terraces. This is why at Mammoth, springs typically come to the surface, flow a short distance and sink again into subterranean channels that have been created where cooler waters have dissolved the travertine.

Chasms where waters can flow back to underground channels are known as sinkholes. Several large sinkholes are protected by fences outside the Mammoth visitor center. Water that flows into these

Liberty Cap stands sentinel over the lower terraces at Mammoth Hot Springs. This now-inactive spring probably flowed from a central vent for many years as it built its impressive cone.

SALVATORE VASAPOLLI

FRED HIRSCHMANN

While vapors rise from hot flowing waters in the background, inactive pools are covered by a light dusting of snow. Although surface expressions of water flow and terrace deposition at Mammoth are remarkable, as much as 90% of the total water flows underground below the terraces.

FRED HIRSCHMANN

DUNCAN FOLEY

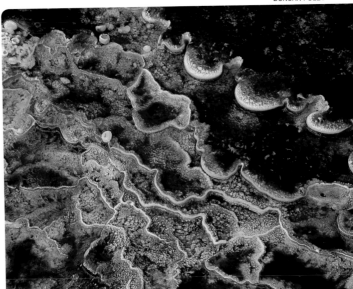

Mammoth is also an excellent area in which to look for small features as well as large ones. The interactions of microbes, water and terraces create unusual patterns in many different colors.

Travertine deposited at Mammoth is very similar to rocks formed in caves. Especially where waters have dripped over terrace edges, stalactite-like rods of travertine can form. Large shelves can collapse, as seen in the background.

sinkholes moves very rapidly. Geologists have discovered that it takes only two hours for water to flow from the sinkholes outside the visitor center to Boiling River along the Gardiner River (approximately one beeline mile north), which is where the thermal waters ultimately discharge from underground to the river.

It is important to note that the bubbling seen at Mammoth is from the carbon dioxide escaping, not true boiling as in geyser systems. The highest temperature measured at Mammoth is less than 167°F (75°C); waters at Mammoth therefore are not hot enough to boil. This is one reason that there are no geysers at Mammoth.

Unlike spring deposits in many geyser basins, travertine at Mammoth typically forms large and small terraces. This may be due to waters flowing over what are initially small irregularities on the ground, which disturb water flow so that travertine

is deposited. Once the initial terraces are formed, they build by continued deposition.

It is easy to tell where surface springs are active at Mammoth; they are brightly colored by different microbes. Areas without water flow have no microbes, and are gray.

Short-term change in the surface features is very common at Mammoth. Scientists have discovered that only about 10% of the water in the Mammoth hydrothermal system actually flows from surface springs where it can be seen. Approximately 90% of the water never reaches the surface but just flows underground to Boiling River. Because only 10% of the water can be seen at the surface, even small changes in the overall water flow in the Mammoth system can result in large changes in surface springs. Despite the 1899 statement that " . . . at Mammoth Hot Springs . . . activity seems not one-tenth that of former times," there does not seem to

Boiling River, downhill from Mammoth, is where most of the surface and subsurface waters of Mammoth discharge into the Gardiner River. It may take as little as two hours for waters from the terraces to reach Boiling River. This is one area where the Park Service has permitted people to soak in thermal waters. But be careful; the waters are hot, and the Gardiner River can be very cold.

be any scientific evidence that flow in the overall hydrothermal system is decreasing.

But Mammoth is outside the caldera, so what is the source of its heat? Geologists once thought that waters from Norris Geyser Basin might be leaking north along a series of major faults that marks the Norris-Mammoth corridor. Now, however, geologists believe that there may be local deep pockets of magma near Mammoth, and that the hot spring waters are relatively local, rather than having traveled from Norris. Of course, it may also be true that the waters at Mammoth are a combination of both Norris and more local waters.

This collapsed, extinct vent area at Mammoth gives a glimpse of what is happening below current hot springs. Waters rise from below through open channels and then flow to the sides, where horizontal deposits of travertine can be seen.

DUNCAN FOLEY

It is easy to see how the Firehole River got its name, as it wends its way through the geysers and hot spring terraces of the Upper Geyser Basin. Vapor can be seen rising from Old Faithful in the background. A prominent trail, which is actually the old main road, curves as it goes past the Old Faithful Inn.

OLD FAITHFUL

Old Faithful, majestic symbol of Yellowstone, is a dramatic geyser that captures the spirit and imagination of visitors. Remarkable in how regular it has been for more than a century, Old Faithful now is changing. But did Old Faithful always erupt every 60 minutes?

Some myths die hard. The best data suggest that Old Faithful never really had a long-term average of exactly an hour between eruptions. The average time between eruptions, notably, has been getting longer in recent years. However, eruption heights have stayed in the same range of about 110 ft to 180 ft (about 30m to 55m) since it was first scientifically observed in the 1870s. And the total amount of water erupted from Old Faithful has apparently stayed in the approximate range of 3,500 to 8,500 gallons (14,000 liters to 32,000 liters).

Look carefully at Old Faithful and you will see that the current smaller cone from which the geyser erupts is built upon broad, gently sloping silica deposits from older springs and geysers. Old Faithful is not the first hot spring or geyser on the hill; it is just the most recent. Several mounds from older springs and geysers can be seen rising from the broad Old Faithful knoll.

Scientists have discovered that a lodgepole pine forest, similar to the forest now surrounding this area, once grew on the broad Old Faithful mound. A hot spring broke through the ground and killed this forest, probably about 700 years ago. The large knobs on the northeast side of Old Faithful's vent may be silica-coated stumps from old trees. The cone of Old Faithful is built upon deposits from this hot spring, and the wonderful geyser activity we see today may be as young as only a few hundred years.

Old Faithful is especially dramatic in the cold of winter. Since hydrothermal features are driven by underground heat and water, changes in air temperature between summer and winter seem to have no influence on their eruption patterns. However, high winds or low atmospheric pressures may slightly alter the eruptions of a few geysers.

FRED HIRSCHMANN

Many people now comment that Old Faithful is no longer as faithful as they have heard. A 1939 report noted that visitors of the time were making the same comments. In the 1870s, the average interval between eruptions of Old Faithful was reported by different people to be 45 to 70 minutes, with more reliable reports being in the general range of 64 to 67 minutes. Recently the average interval has been slightly longer than 90 minutes, which is much greater than during the 1870s. But what does "average" now mean?

One interesting fact about Old Faithful is that since the 1959 earthquake, it typically has not had "average" intervals and durations. It either has had short eruptions (lasting about 2 minutes) or it has had long eruptions (lasting about 4 minutes or more); "average" eruptions have been uncommon. In general, short duration eruptions have been followed by short intervals to the next eruption (often about 65 minutes), and long duration eruptions have been followed by long intervals to the next eruption (typically more than 90 minutes). This relationship between duration and interval until the next eruption forms the basis upon which park service personnel make forecasts of the time of the next eruption.

But why have these changes occurred? Old Faithful responds, as do other geysers, to plumbing changes that result from fractures being opened or closed by ground shaking from earthquakes (espe-cially in 1959 and 1983) and from sealing of small channels by deposition of silica. The force of eruptions may also fracture the plumbing. The ongoing conflicts between geologic processes that open fractures and geologic processes that seal and close fractures lead to dynamic changes. Indeed, it is amazing that, even with its changes, that Old Faithful has been so faithful so long.

EXPLOSIONS WITHOUT MAGMA

Can there be explosions that don't involve magma? If conditions are just right, small eruptions can be caused by the explosive force of water changing to steam, without any new magma coming out at the surface. These are called phreatic (pronounced "free-attic") or hydrothermal eruptions or explosions. Yellowstone, with its subterranean water and heat, has had many hydrothermal explosions in the past 15,000 years.

Hydrothermal explosions are geologically similar to what would happen if you took the top off a hot pressure cooker in your kitchen (please don't do this; the explosion of overpressured water to steam will cause severe burns!). A pressure cooker works by having a lid that clamps down and raises the pressure inside the pot. Raising the pressure causes the boiling temperature of the water inside to become greater. If the pressure cooker lid is suddenly removed, the pressure drops quickly, and the higher temperature water instantly explodes to steam.

ROBERT FOURNIER

Wall Pool and *Black Opal Pool in Biscuit Basin sit quietly now, but the scattered rocks between the pools and the Firehole River suggest a violent past. The rocks were blown out when a hydrothermal explosion formed the crater in 1925. Subsequent explosions in the winter of 1931 and 1932 enlarged the pool.*

Monkey flowers, which like to grow in moist or wet areas, line the channel of this thermal spring at Terrace Spring near Madison Junction. Microclimates near thermal features can extend the growing season for plants.

ROBERT FOURNIER

Thermal pools in Yellowstone are teeming with *microscopic* life!

Mother nature and father time can also work like the pressure cooker. Geologic environments that can create hydrothermal explosions require underground systems where high pressures can suddenly be lowered (removing the lid) and high temperature water can be explosively converted to steam. Geologically, lids that trap high temperature water can be formed by covering an area with water (as under a lake) or by creating a mineral seal at the top of a hydrothermal system.

But how can a lake drain suddenly enough to trigger an explosion? One possibility is that a lake could be dammed by ice during an ice age. At the end of the ice age, the dam would break during

ROBERT FOURNIER

Small mud cones can look like miniature volcanoes, complete with mud flows down their sides that are reminiscent of lava flows from larger volcanoes.

- 39 -

Fishing Cone at West Thumb
*Geyser Basin is one of the most
famous hydrothermal features in Yellowstone.
Hot waters that rise through the center
of the cone are almost completely isolated
from the surrounding cold lake water.
Early visitors told tales of catching trout
in the lake and cooking them in the cone.*

melting. This would suddenly lower the lake, and the high temperature hydrothermal system under the lake bottom could suddenly explode and form a crater. This is thought to be how Pocket Basin, in the Lower Geyser Basin, formed.

An underground mineral seal can also act as a lid and raise the pressure and therefore the boiling temperature of a hydrothermal system. If the seal is broken, perhaps by being shaken by an earthquake, the system can explode. This may be how Indian Pond and Mary Bay at Yellowstone Lake formed.

Geysers can also create hydrothermal explosions. Porkchop Geyser in the Back Basin at Norris Geyser Basin was a perpetual spouter that kept building up pressure until it exploded in September 1989. The debris around the rim of Porkchop is still impressive as seen from the boardwalk, and it is easy to imagine the explosive nature of its eruption.

The combination of heat, water and minerals means that Yellowstone is primed for future hydrothermal explosions. Will West Thumb of Yellowstone Lake be the next hydrothermal explosion? Or will it be Mary Bay, also at the lake? These areas are hot at their bottoms, and the overlying lake water acts as the lid on a pressure cooker. Or will it be somewhere else, such as rapidly changing Norris Geyser Basin?

OLD ROOTS AND NEW DISCOVERIES

New scientific tools and techniques are opening new worlds of discovery about Yellowstone and its hydrothermal systems. A few years ago very little was known about the bottom of Yellowstone Lake. Now new mapping techniques are being used, and this deep, dark world is being revealed as one of the most fascinating and complex areas in the park. New breakthroughs in studying microbes are opening our eyes to the fascinating world of hot-spring-loving life forms, which may, in their own way, tell us much about the origin of life on Earth.

YELLOWSTONE LAKE

Fishing Cone and Lakeshore Geyser at West Thumb can astound viewers. It is easy to understand how geysers, surrounded by land, can have hot waters make it to the surface. But geysers surrounded

Duck Lake lies adjacent to the West Thumb Geyser Basin, portions of which can be seen along the shoreline of Yellowstone Lake at the bottom of the photograph. Duck Lake is one of several hydrothermal explosion craters in Yellowstone. These craters are created by an explosion of highly pressured water to steam, without the eruption of new magma. Fires during 1988 burned the trees but did not impact hydrothermal features.

DUNCAN FOLEY

by a cold lake? These are dramatic evidence of hot waters rising along fractures that are separated from cold waters.

Fishing Cone and Lakeshore Geyser, although unusual, are just tantalizing hints of the vast underwater world of hydrothermal features that is now being discovered at the bottom of the lake. Although it has been known for decades that the bottom of the lake was hot in some places, only in the past few years have fields of underwater hot springs and numerous lake-floor hydrothermal explosion craters been identified.

Some geologists estimate that as many as 10% of Yellowstone's hydrothermal systems may be lurking under the lake. How big these systems are, how much water they discharge, and even the locations of all the systems are still being discovered. New ways of sampling and mapping the bottom of the 430 ft (131m) deep lake, however, are helping explore this new frontier.

Beach Springs, by the road along the shore of Mary Bay, hint at another remarkable aspect of the hydrothermal story of Yellowstone Lake. These are 199°F (93°C) springs that bubble and hiss from the sands along the lakeshore. Small trails of bubbles can also be seen rising through the lake water when the bay is calm. Overall, these quiet springs provide little hint of the violent origin of Mary Bay, which is a coalesced series of hydrothermal explosion craters (not a volcanic magmatic crater) that has been filled in by lake waters. The hills along the east and northeast sides of Mary Bay are debris from the eruption.

SANDRA NYKERK

This quiet thermal pond near Yellowstone Lake belies the violent origin of Mary Bay. The hills in the background are debris that rims a major hydrothermal explosion crater, which occurred about 13,000 years ago.

Chaotic rock and sediment fragments from this eruption can be seen in the steep road cut at Steamboat Point.

Where the bottom of the lake is hot, the potential for new hydrothermal explosions exists (but the chances of one occurring during your visit are vanishingly small). Both Mary Bay and West Thumb have hot waters rising through their lake-bottom

SANDRA NYKERK

Iron and arsenic color the geyser deposits in the outflow channel of Echinus Geyser in Norris Geyser Basin. Trees that are caught in the outflow channel will be covered by new rocks and buried.

FRED HIRSCHMANN

Hot spring microbes form the basis of a food chain. Eurypterid flies, such as these swarming around a cooler portion of an outflow channel, feed on the microbes. The flies occupy an intermediate level in the food chain, as they are fed upon by birds.

sediments, and some geologists feel that these two sites may have future eruptions.

A smaller hydrothermal explosion crater can be seen at Indian Pond, which is south of the main road slightly west of Beach Springs. Duck Lake, in the woods west of West Thumb, is another easily seen hydrothermal explosion crater.

Even with the new discoveries, many mysteries remain about the underwater hydrothermal systems. In the past few years, spires of up to 25 ft (8 m) tall have been discovered in the northern part of the lake. How did they form? What do they tell us about other spires, such as those in Monument Basin south of Gibbon Meadow? What other geologic secrets still lie beneath the lake's waters?

LIFE IN HOT WATER

Do Yellowstone hot springs hold the key to life on Mars? Is there a clue to a cure for skin cancer in the brightly colored channels that flow from the springs? Do Yellowstone microbes come close to the origin of life on Earth?

Visitors remark with awe at the brilliant reds, oranges and greens that color spring outflow channels. Many of these colors owe their origin not to minerals deposited from spring waters, but to different types of algae, bacteria and archaea that live at different temperatures in the waters. Known as thermophiles, these are microorganisms that have the

ability to live at temperatures that would easily kill a human.

As amazing as it may seem, even the clearest, hottest waters in thermal pools in Yellowstone are teeming with microscopic life.

Microbes that thrive in different temperature waters create the characteristic color changes in outflow channels of hot springs. The hottest waters are clear, and as they flow away from springs and cool, often first bright yellows, oranges and reds are found, with green colors typical of cooler waters.

The DNA Story at Yellowstone

The microbes of Yellowstone are far from being just objects of scientific curiosity. They have many practical applications, and may yet be the source of billion-dollar industries. The technique of DNA fingerprinting, which has been made famous in criminal trials, is based on *Thermous aquaticus*, a microbe first identified from Mushroom Spring in the Lower Geyser Basin. In food processing, baking, brewing and almost any place in industry where high temperatures are encountered and enzymes can be used, there may be new roles for Yellowstone's microbes.

Study of Yellowstone's microbes will increase our understanding of life itself. Can it be, as some scientists have suggested, that the diversity of life in Octopus Pool near Great Fountain Geyser in the Lower Geyser Basin, just one of Yellowstone's more than 10,000 hydrothermal features, is greater than the diversity of life in a tropical rain forest? Scientists used specialized biological techniques to discover that the colored mats, once thought to be composed largely of single organisms, are instead composed of complex communities of organisms. Some members of these communities may be closely related to what scientists think were the earliest forms of life on earth. Other communities have microbes that are closely related to microbes that live in the lightless deep-sea hydrothermal vents.

When you look at the brilliant colors in hot waters in geyser basins, think for a moment about what secrets are yet to be discovered in the microscopic world that lies at your feet.

DUNCAN FOLEY

Green colors in acidic thermal waters, such as these of Nymph Creek between Mammoth and Norris, can often indicate a microbial community characterized by the algae *Cyanidium*. This microbe is highly unusual, as it can survive in heat and acidity that would kill most other organisms.

DUNCAN FOLEY

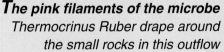

The pink filaments of the microbe *Thermocrinus Ruber* drape around the small rocks in this outflow channel. These filaments are found only in one channel of this hot spring, where the microbes live in the narrow temperature range of about 80 – 87 degrees C (about 175 to 190 degrees F).

Interpreting What You See

How can you tell what are you looking at? Is it a hot spring, a geyser, a fumarole or a mud pot? Is water or steam rising through underground fractures?

In hot springs and geysers, liquid water is dominant as the rising fluid. In fumaroles and mud pots, steam is dominant as the rising fluid.

It can be difficult to tell inactive geysers from hot springs. One clue in identifying a feature can be the shape of silica deposits around its rim. At a hot spring, there may be a very delicate thin rim of silica formed out over the edge of the pool. The violent eruption of an exploding geyser will typically destroy such a feature. A hot spring may also have very brightly colored bands of bacteria growing on their margins, while the bacteria might not survive if upwelling geyser waters swamp them. Geyser runout channels, however, will often be colored from bacteria. A geyser also may build a cone, such as Castle, Giant or Beehive in the Upper Geyser Basin.

In vapor-dominated areas, smell may be the first way to detect rising steam. Especially at sites such as Mud Volcano, the rotten egg odor of hydrogen sulphide gas often will be smelled even before any hydrothermal features can be seen.

Fumaroles and mudpots are common in vapor-dominated areas. They can be distinguished by their output. Fumaroles just emit gas, so if you hear a hissing noise but see no water, you probably are looking at a fumarole. Mudpots will bubble and blurp small to large amounts of mud, but will have little or no water run off.

FRED HIRSCHMANN

Hot spring or geyser? The thick ledge of sinter over the pool suggests hot spring, as the edge would likely be broken in a geyser eruption.

FRED HIRSCHMANN

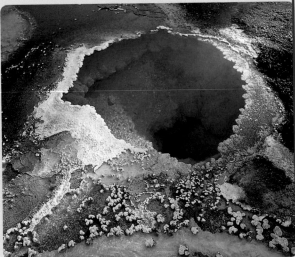

Hot spring or geyser? The delicate scalloping around the edge of this pool suggests that it is a hot spring.

Hot spring or geyser? Silex Spring, in the Lower Geyser Basin, usually flows calmly but occasionally it will erupt.

SANDRA NYKERK

Your Safety and Yellowstone's Future

Preservation of Yellowstone's hydrothermal systems is up to you, as is safety when enjoying these dangerous features. Please do nothing to disturb the sites. Do not throw objects, such as coins, into the pools. Never take pets into thermal areas. The algae and bacteria have a difficult life living in the changing outflow channels. Please do not deface these mats, as even innocent markings can last for many years. Do not smoke or litter in thermal areas. Litter can blow into the pools or geysers, and help choke them off.

It is important to stay on marked boardwalks and trails. Many areas have thin crusts with boiling waters only a few inches or feet below you. In these areas, ground surface temperatures can be very high. Looking alone is not enough to tell if a crust can hold your weight or not. Be very careful, and supervise children closely.

Although people may think we know best where to locate boardwalks, nature sometimes has other ideas. This is Bastille Geyser, which erupted for a short time right beside a boardwalk in Norris Geyser Basin. This boardwalk has since been removed, as new thermal outbreaks have impacted several other portions of it.

DUNCAN FOLEY

All About Yellowstone's Geysers & Hydrothermal Features

How to Contact Us:

Call us at
(307) 344-7381

Write to us at:
Yellowstone National Park
P.O. Box 168
Yellowstone, WY 82190

Local Radio for Park Information
AM1610

Visit us at our Website:
www.nps.gov/yell

The Yellowstone Natural History Association, a non-profit organization, has been a partner in the education of park visitors since 1933. The Association funds projects ranging from training for the park's interpretive rangers to providing exhibits and films for the park's visitor centers using proceeds from sales of educational materials in park visitor centers and contributions from its members. Each year, the organization's Yellowstone Association Institute provides hundreds of field courses and seminars to thousands of park visitors.

New Geyser Visitor Center

Educational opportunities for park visitors about hydrothermal systems are greatly enhanced by the new Old Faithful Visitor Education Center. The multistory building includes interactive exhibits about Yellowstone's hydrothermal features. The story of Old Faithful is augmented by stories about other hydrothermal systems and their associated life forms.

SUGGESTED READING

Bryan, T. Scott. *Geysers of Yellowstone.* Boulder, Colorado: University Press of Colorado, 2003.

Bryan, T. Scott. *Geysers – What They Are and How They Work.* Missoula, Montana: Mountain Press, 2005.

Sheehan, Kathy B., David L. Patterson, Brett L. Dicks and Joan M. Henson. *Seen and Unseen, Discovering the Microbes of Yellowstone.* Helena, Montana: Falcon Press, 2005.

Smith, Robert L. and Lee J. Siegel. *Windows into the Earth.* New York: Oxford University Press, 2000.

Places to see:

Boiling River

Mammoth Hot Springs

Roaring Mountain

Canyon

Norris Geyser Basin

Chocolate Pots

Gibbon Falls

Mud Volcano

Mary Bay

Lower Geyser Basin

Midway Geyser Basin

Biscuit Basin

Black Sand Basin

Upper Geyser Basin

Steamboat Point

West Thumb

Bechler (back country)

SUGGESTED WEB SITES

www.nps.gov/yell/nature/geothermal
www.geyserstudy.org/geyser_main.htm
http://volcanoes.usgs.gov/yvo/

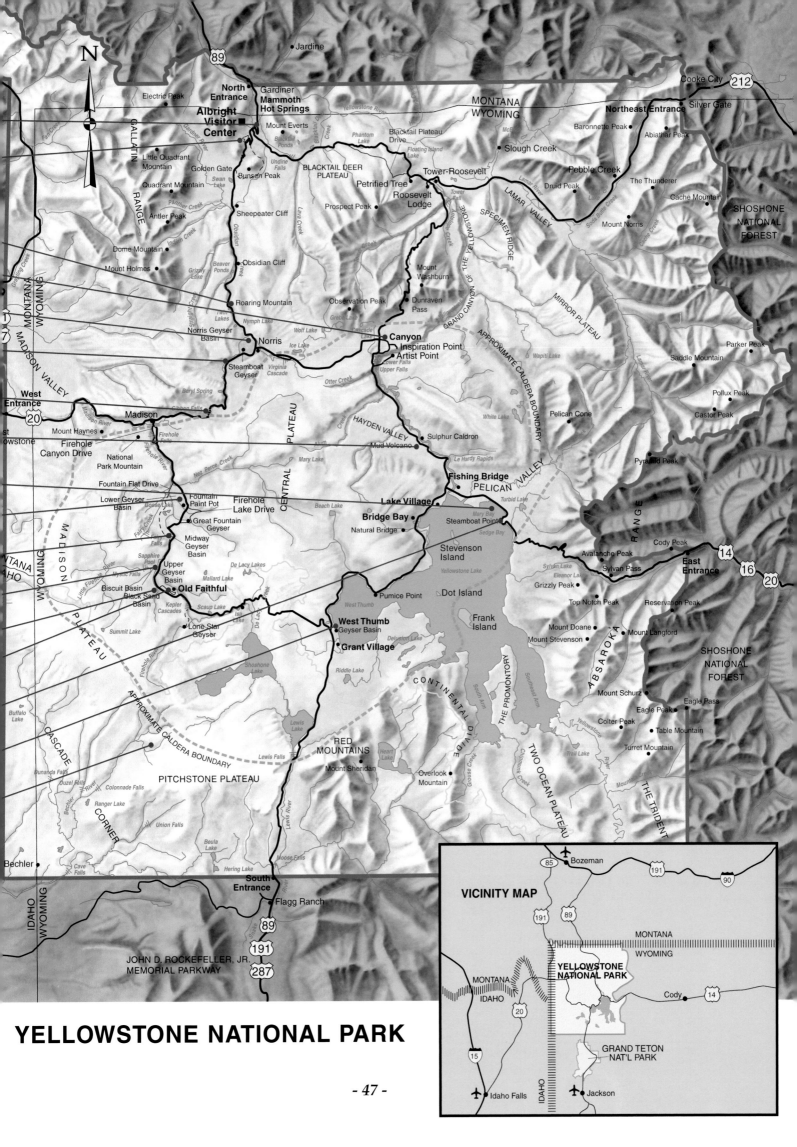

YELLOWSTONE NATIONAL PARK

A Look To The Future

Careful stewardship by humans has resulted in the continued existence of Yellowstone's hydrothermal systems. For more than a century we have chosen to protect this area because of these magnificent features. We need to continue to choose, as individuals and as a nation, to preserve these powerful yet fragile demonstrations of nature's majesty.

The amazing geological world of Yellowstone's thermal features has been a source of awe for generations. There are fountains of water that shoot high in the air and deep blue pools, too hot to touch.

White and gray pots of exploding mud accompany vents with rushing gasses. Brilliant orange, green and white channels, colored by microscopic creatures that reach back to the beginning of life on earth, drain these remarkable features. Volcanic rocks are cooked to brilliant white, shimmering yellow, iron red and deepest black. We have listened, probed, measured and observed to learn about geysers, mud pots, hot springs and fumaroles, but in the dynamic world of geology in Yellowstone, there is much more yet to be discovered.

JOHN P. GEORGE

Great Fountain Geyser, in the Lower Geyser Basin, is a pool type geyser that has built broad terraces.

KC Publications has been the leading publisher of colorful, interpretive books about National Park areas, public lands, Indian lands, and related subjects for over 43 years. We have 6 active series—over 125 titles—with Translation Packages in up to 8 languages for over half the areas we cover. Write, call, or visit our web site for our full-color catalog.

Our series are:

The Story Behind the Scenery® – Compelling stories of over 65 National Park areas and similar Public Land areas. Some with Translation Packages.

in pictures... The Continuing Story® – A companion, pictorially oriented, series on America's National Parks. All titles have Translation Packages.

For Young Adventurers® – Dedicated to young seekers and keepers of all things wild and sacred. Explore America's Heritage from A to Z.

Voyage of Discovery® – Exploration of the expansion of the western United States.

Indian Culture and the Southwest – All about Native Americans, past and present.

Calendars – For National Parks in dramatic full color, and a companion Color Your Own series, with crayons.

To receive our full-color catalog featuring over 125 titles—Books, Calendars, and other related specialty products:
Call (800-626-9673), fax (702-433-3420), write to the address below, or visit our web sites at www.kcpub.com and www.kcspeaks.com

Published by KC Publications, 3245 E. Patrick Ln., Suite A, Las Vegas, NV 89120.

Inside Back Cover: Sunrise and sunset are excellent times to enjoy the geyser basins. Photo by Erwin & Peggy Bauer / Wildstock.

Back Cover: Terraces of Canary Hot Spring, Mammoth. Photo by Fred Hirschmann.

Created, Designed, and Published in the U.S.A.
Printed by Tien Wah Press (Pte.) Ltd, Singapore
Color Separations by United Graphic Pte. Ltd

CANADIAN Snapshots

STUDENT BOOK

Linking to the Community

STUDENT BOOK

CANADIAN
Snapshots

KATHY ANGST

CHRISTINE BERTRAM

MARY JEAN DAVIS

LINDA JOHANSSON

FRANCIS J. BONKOWSKI

Linking to the Community

PEARSON
Longman ESL

DISTRIBUTED IN CANADA BY ERPI

5757, RUE CYPIHOT, SAINT-LAURENT (QUÉBEC) H4S 1R3
TELEPHONE: (514) 334-2690 ext. 232   FAX: (514) 334-0448
infoesl@erpi.com   www.longmanesl.ca

ACKNOWLEDGEMENTS

The authors would like to thank:

- Joanne Pettis who provided the initial spark of leadership and inspiration;

- Dr. David Mendelsohn, York University, ON (pedagogical consultant);

- Gail Tiessen, Providence Seminary, MA (pedagogical consultant);

- Jean-Pierre Albert, Vice-President Publishing, Pearson Longman ESL Canada;

- Sharnee Chait for her support and encouragement;

- Our original team members: Mavis Harper, who provided our initial technical support, Frances Molaro, and Lisa Petit;

- Our colleagues and students from the Winnipeg School Division Adult ESL Program.

Finally, a very special note of thanks to our families for their love and support:

- Sarah, John and Bob Angst;

- Stephen, Laurie, Andrea and Laurence Bertram;

- Brian, Grant and Bob Davis;

- Anders, Evan, Karin and Gert Johansson;

- Andrea, Valérie and Jacqueline Froidefond.

We'd like to dedicate this book to adult ESL learners who are our inspiration.

© 2005 Longman Published and distributed by
ÉDITIONS DU RENOUVEAU PÉDAGOGIQUE INC.
All rights reserved.

Registration of copyright: 1st quarter 2005
Bibliothèque nationale du Québec
National Library of Canada
Printed in Canada

ISBN 2-7613-1434-4

CREDITS

p. 33 photograph courtesy of the Canadian MedicAlert® Foundation. (MedicAlert is a registered trademark and service mark.) p. 60 photograph © Dorling Kindersly; p. 61 photograph © Pearson Education - PH College

Editor: Sharnee Chait

Developmental editor: Francis J. Bonkowski

Production supervisor: Muriel Normand

Cover: Marie-Hélène Martel

Book design and art coordination: Frédérique Bouvier

Page layout: 4b communication

Illustrations: Anthony Baker

ABOUT THE AUTHORS

Kathy Angst, **Christine Bertram**, **Mary Jean Davis** and **Linda Johansson** have extensive experience in various dimensions of adult ESL and ESL literacy instruction. Since 1996, they have been involved in various aspects of implementation of the Canadian Language Benchmarks provincially on behalf of Manitoba Labour and Immigration, Adult Language Training Branch, including curriculum resource development and pilot projects. Following the release of the *Canadian Language Benchmarks 2000*, they developed supplemental material for the Centre for Canadian Language Benchmarks, in particular, *Canadian Language Benchmarks 2000: ESL for Literacy Learners*. Currently, the authors work in the Adult ESL Program delivered by Winnipeg School Division, in Winnipeg, Manitoba.

Francis J. Bonkowski has taught ESL in high school and college. He is a co-author of ESL textbooks (*Take* Collection and the Canadian adaptation of *Thresholds in Reading*) and has designed distance education materials.

1234567890 HLN 098765
131434 ABCD   OF10

INTRODUCTION

Canadian Snapshots: Linking to the Community is an integrated multimedia educational package for Stage 1, Canadian Language Benchmarks Level 3 (high beginner). Using the task-based philosophy provided by the *Canadian Language Benchmarks 2000: A Guide to Implementation* as a frame of reference, each unit provides practical, multi-skill, communicative language tasks that link adult ESL learners with the Canadian community. Special features include culture notes, learning strategies, communicative grammar and pronunciation pointers. The resource package includes the Student Book, Workbook, Audio Program, Companion Website and Instructor's Manual.

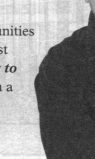

"Bringing about effective change takes time and requires opportunities for teachers to become familiar with the content, issues, and best practices of the new direction."* ***Canadian Snapshots: Linking to the Community*** will provide new and experienced teachers with a way to incorporate content and communicative language skills within the Canadian Language Benchmarks framework.

* Canadian Language Benchmarks 2000: A Guide to Implementation, p. 2

STUDENT BOOK

The Student Book contains ten units which follow a similar pattern.

Goals and language functions are listed at the beginning of each unit.

At the end of the unit, this review gives learners the tools to self-assess their progress.

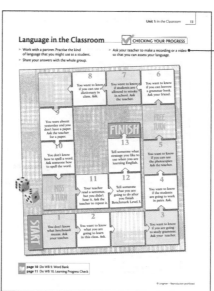

A picture and a paragraph help learners to focus on the theme and the specific language they will need.

Talking It Over allows learners to describe what they see, think about the situation and predict what will happen.

How About You? encourages learners to create meaning from their past experience and knowledge.

Words to Think About introduces words that students will learn throughout the unit.

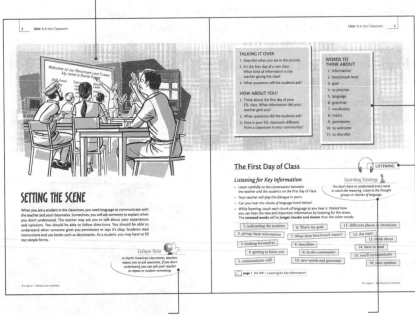

Learners listen to realistic language for different kinds of information.

Listening for Key Information teaches learners how to listen for chunks of language.

Listening for Details guides learners to listen for specific information.

Listening for the Gist provides practice in listening for the message.

Culture notes help learners be aware of ways of thinking, feeling and behaving within the Canadian community.

The development of learning strategies can allow language learners to be more productive, successful and self-directed.

Reading text is based on authentic, realistic reading tasks, covering social interaction, instructions, business/service and information.

Learners are taught how to write by reading and discussing a model (a form, a story or a letter).

Students learn to speak within a guided and meaningful framework, linked to the pronunciation and grammar skill-building exercises.

Vocabulary that is needed to talk about the topic is presented and practised in different ways.

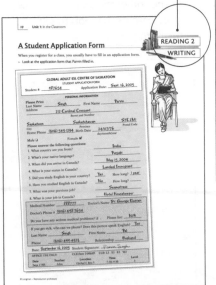

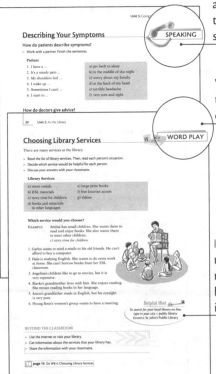

Helpful hints provide learners with more information. Another special margin note, Feel Empowered, offers learners a valuable expression to use in specific situations.

This section helps learners to understand and organize how English language functions.

develop an awareness of how learners can improve their pronunciation so that people can understand them more clearly.

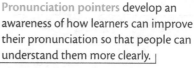

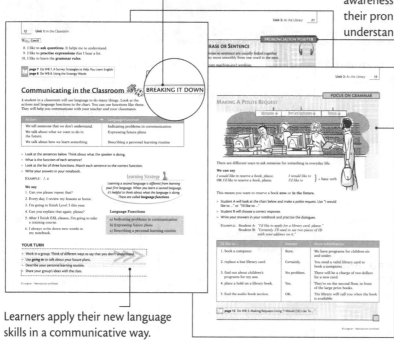

Focus on Grammar points are based on the language functions needed to complete the communicative tasks, with opportunities for skill-building and then skill-using.

Learners apply their new language skills in a communicative way.

WORKBOOK

Exercises in the workbook develop the skills introduced in the Student Book. They provide practice and a chance to implement the language skills in a purposeful, meaningful and often communicative way.

The learner reads the completed form in the Student Book and fills out a form in the Workbook.

RESOURCE PACKAGE

Audio Program

For each unit, there are:
- recorded dialogues used to introduce each topic;
- listening activities based on the dialogue in each unit;
- a pronunciation exercise related to the topic.

Instructor's Manual

Support for teachers includes procedures for classroom activities, transcripts of all recorded material and further suggestions.

Canadian Snapshots Companion Website

Each unit has four self-correcting activities to strengthen the various language skills and to self-assess learning. A teacher's section has annotated links to outside websites with suggestions for activities.

SCOPE AND OVERVIEW

	SPEAKING	LISTENING	READING
Unit 1 **In the Classroom**	Ask for help, permission or an explanation. Describe goals. Ask about and describe personal learning strategies.	Understand a teacher's explanation. Respond to expressions of permission.	Read: - a letter from the teacher - a student application form
Unit 2 **At the Library**	Respond to an offer of assistance by library staff. Ask library staff how to access services. Give directions to locate library materials and services.	Follow directions to locate sections and services.	Read and follow a floor plan. Read guidelines and a library card application form.
Unit 3 **Going to the Doctor**	Describe health problems.	Understand when the doctor greets you and says goodbye. Respond to medical advice and questions.	Read: - a prescription label - a fitness class schedule - a short personal experience Use the Yellow Pages.
Unit 4 **In the Supermarket**	Ask for assistance in a supermarket. Clarify position and location of items and sections.	Follow directions to locate items.	Find information on labels and a coupon. Read a store membership card. Read about shopping experiences.
Unit 5 **Reporting a Medical Emergency**	Request 9-1-1 assistance. Describe an emergency situation.	Understand and follow instructions from a 9-1-1 operator. Understand and respond to emergency advice and warnings.	Read: - a phone directory for steps in an emergency - a pamphlet - an accident report form

WRITING	STRATEGIES	CULTURE	LANGUAGE FEATURES
Fill out a student application form. Write a short text about a personal situation.	Listen for chunks of language. Understand language functions. Listen for question words. Reread to find/check information. Check for accuracy in forms.	Asking teacher if you don't understand Formality of teacher names Understanding when permission is necessary Filling in all sections of a form Classroom protocol	Modal *can* *Going to* for future plans Pitch direction of questions Format of a letter Format of a form
Fill in a library card application form.	Use landmarks for orientation. Use body language for directions.	Library rules Library services and programs	Prepositions of location Courtesy formulas *I'd like to* Linking words in a phrase or sentence Layout of a map Format of a form Directional symbols Models *can* and *could* Time markers
Fill out a medical history.	Listen for important words. Locate information using guide words in alphabetical order. Use a writing model.	MedicAlert and allergies Medical services Telephone directory Importance of medical history	Greetings and leave takings Modal *should* Word stress Adjectives Format of a label, schedule, directory, form and line graph Past continuous tense
Fill out a store membership card application. Describe and compare shopping in another country or community.	Listen for question words. Use body language. Repeat for clarification. Use headings to locate information. Follow a model to write a story.	Customer service Sections of a supermarket Returning items Use of coupons, unit pricing and store membership cards Expiry date and nutrition labels	Prepositions of location Question making Lip rounding Comparative adjectives Format of paragraphs Time markers
Fill out: - an accident report - a hospital admissions form	Use landmarks to describe locations. Listen for pitch in conversations. Repeat questions if you don't understand. Locate key information with guide words, bold print and underlining.	Ambulance service fees Emergency payphone calls Street addresses and apartment numbers When to call 9-1-1 Importance of accident report	Imperatives Major sentence stress Past tense with *just* Question making Symbols for 9-1-1 Emergency Services Date Format

	SPEAKING	LISTENING	READING
Unit 6 **Dealing with Consumer Problems**	Describe a problem about a purchase. Ask for an explanation of a service or product. Return product and ask for service.	Understand: - questions and answers from customer service reps - offers of assistance Understand and respond to a direct salesperson.	Read: - store policy signs - a warranty - a warranty registration card - a letter of complaint
Unit 7 **Getting Ready to Look for Work**	Describe skills, experience, job duties and employment goals. Give work preferences.	Listen and respond to employment counsellor's interview questions. Listen and choose a preference.	Find information in a registration form for employment counselling.
Unit 8 **Applying for Work**	Request information about a job. Ask for an application form.	Follow directions to pick up a job application.	Read: - job ads - instructions in an application form - a pie chart
Unit 9 **Lifelong Learning**	Talk about: - positive and negative feelings - a course you want to take - equipment and supplies for the course	Get details from a phone message.	Find information in a community activity guide and a receipt.
Unit 10 **Getting Ready for a Job Interview**	Begin and end a conversation. Express future plans. Ask for an explanation. Describe skills and abilities. Describe employment goals. Talk about occupations and work experience.	Listen and respond to questions.	Read and follow instructions. Read: - job ads and postings - a resume

WRITING	STRATEGIES	CULTURE	LANGUAGE FEATURES
Fill out a warranty registration card. Write a letter of complaint.	Listen for: - the first word in Yes/No questions - common expressions Repeat questions to see if you understand. Follow a model for writing a letter. Write short notes to remember details.	Return policies Appropriate responses to direct salespeople Keeping receipts and warranty cards Importance of reading the fine print	If-clause with *will* Yes/No questions Syllables and rhythm Format of warranties and guarantees Letter format
Fill out an employment agency registration form.	Set goals. Use tips to fill out forms.	Job search services and resources Resume Volunteer work experience	Questions with the modal *can* Word stress and *-tion* endings *Prefer* with gerund/infinitive *Because of* to give reasons
Fill out a job application form. Label and fill in a chart. Write a cover letter.	Skim for details. Use a dictionary for new words and spelling.	Importance of intonation Correct titles (*Mr.*, *Mrs.*, *Ms.*) Job references Networking process Sections of an application form	Indefinite pronouns Linking sounds Adjectives Adverbs Format of pamphlets Abbreviations Format of a formal letter
Record details from an activity guide. Write a thank-you note.	Make notes while listening to a message. Use a model to write a letter or note. Use key words to get the main idea.	Continuing education and community activity guides Registration and refund process	Adjectives Meaning of *need to* and *want to* Blended sounds Format of a guide, receipt and an informal note Capitalization
Fill in a form. Write a simple business memo. Prepare a resume.	Ask or repeat questions if you don't understand. Write short notes to remember details. Use a model for writing. Use a dictionary or ask someone if you don't understand words. Practise before a job interview.	Resume writing Positive personal qualities of job applicants	Greetings and leave takings Recognition and use of intonation in conversation

TABLE OF CONTENTS

In the Classroom

Learning Opportunities

Can you communicate with your teacher and classmates? Do you know how to ask for help in the class? Do you have the language that you need to explain your goals? Can you answer questions about what you want to learn and how you like to learn? Do you know strategies that will make learning easier? In this unit, you will learn:

- To indicate problems in communication.
- To express future plans.
- To describe ways to learn.
- To identify expressions to grant permission.
- To get the gist about a daily routine from a short letter.
- To read a short letter for important information.
- To fill out simple forms.
- To write a short text about a personal situation.

UNIT 1

SETTING THE SCENE

When you are a student in the classroom, you need language to communicate with the teacher and your classmates. Sometimes, you will ask someone to explain when you don't understand. The teacher may ask you to talk about your experiences and opinions. You should be able to follow directions. You should be able to understand when someone gives you permission or says it's okay. Students read instructions and use books such as dictionaries. As a student, you may have to fill out simple forms.

Culture Note

In North American classrooms, teachers expect you to ask questions. If you don't understand, you can ask your teacher to repeat or explain something.

TALKING IT OVER

1. Describe what you see in the picture.

2. It's the first day of a new class. What kind of information is the teacher giving the class?

3. What questions will the students ask?

HOW ABOUT YOU?

1. Think about the first day of your ESL class. What information did your teacher give you?

2. What questions did the students ask?

3. How is your ESL classroom different from a classroom in your community?

WORDS TO THINK ABOUT

1. information
2. benchmark level
3. goal
4. to practise
5. language
6. grammar
7. vocabulary
8. topics
9. permission
10. to welcome
11. to describe

The First Day of Class

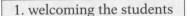 LISTENING

Listening for Key Information

➤ Listen carefully to the conversation between the teacher and the students on the first day of class.

➤ Your teacher will play the dialogue in parts.

➤ Can you hear the *chunks of language* listed below?

➤ While listening, touch each chunk of language as you hear it. Notice how you can hear the new and important information by listening for the stress. The **stressed words** will be **longer, louder and slower** than the other words.

Learning Strategy

You don't have to understand every word to catch the meaning. Listen to the thought groups or chunks of language.

1. welcoming the students
2. giving them information
3. looking forward to
4. getting to know you
5. communicate well
6. That's my goal.
7. What does *benchmark* mean?
8. describes
9. in the community
10. new words and grammar
11. different places or situations
12. the topic
13. think about
14. have to read
15. you'll communicate
16. your opinion

 page 1 Do WB 1. Listening for Key Information

Cont'd

Listening for Details

➤ Read the following questions. Think about what information you need to answer each question.

➤ Listen to the dialogue. Number from 1 to 8 in your notebook. Write down one or two words to answer each question. Use the Listening Strategy below.

➤ Discuss your answers.

1. When does this dialogue take place?

2. What benchmark level is this class?

3. Should the students call their teacher Mrs. Rogers?

4. Do the students understand everything the teacher says?

5. Where are the students going to use their English?

6. What do some students want to study?

7. Are the students going to work in groups?

8. What does the teacher want the students to do?

Learning Strategy ♟

Listening for Question Words

Listen for question words: *Who, What, When,* etc. Ask yourself "What kind of specific information am I listening for?" Try to find out:

◆ *Who* is speaking? Who is the person speaking to?

◆ *What* is it about? (an idea, a plan, a situation)

◆ *When* is it? (before, now, later on)

◆ *Where* is it? (a place, a location)

◆ *Why* is this happening? (a reason or an explanation)

◆ *What* are the key words and verbs in the question?

◆ *What* is the relationship between the speakers?

◆ *What* is the mood or atmosphere?

YOUR TURN

➤ Work with a partner. Use the list of questions about the dialogue.

➤ Practise asking each other these questions about the first day of ESL class.

➤ Answer the questions with a couple of words or a phrase.

EXAMPLE: Student A: *"What benchmark level is this class?"*
Student B: *"Benchmark Level 3."*

Listening for the Gist

Getting Permission

As a student, you may have to ask for permission in certain situations.
You need the language to understand when you *have permission*.
You need the language to understand when you *don't have permission*.

> *Sure. You can smoke outside.* → Giving permission
> *Sorry. You can't smoke in the building.* → Not giving permission

➤ Listen to the dialogue. You will hear a student asking for permission to do something. Then you will hear the teacher's response.

➤ Is the teacher giving permission or not giving permission? Is the teacher saying "yes" or "no"?

➤ Discuss your choices with your classmates.

 page 2 Do WB 2. Getting Permission in Classroom Situations

Asking Questions in the ESL Classroom SPEAKING

a) What does _____ mean?

b) Can you help me?

c) May I borrow an _____ please?

d) Can you explain that please?

e) How do you spell this word?

f) How do you pronounce this word?

g) Can you repeat that please?

h) Can you speak slowly please?

i) Can you show me how to ...?

j) May I have a _____ please?

Can You...?

➤ Read the questions on the board in the illustration.

➤ Match one of the questions to each situation described below.

➤ Write your answers in your notebook. Compare your answers with a partner. Practise saying each question out loud.

Learning Strategy

Look for a word in the situation and use it in the question.

EXAMPLE: Mario's teacher said their class is a Benchmark 3. He doesn't understand what *benchmark* means. What question should he ask?

a) What does benchmark mean?

1. Hossein was absent from school yesterday. The class is reviewing yesterday's work. He doesn't have a paper to read.

2. Vivian's teacher is giving directions to an exercise, but Vivian doesn't understand. She needs an explanation.

Cont'd

3. Raquel is writing in her journal. She wants to write a word but she can't spell it.

4. Noor lost his eraser. He wants to borrow one from a classmate.

5. Anna is practising information about her children's school. She has a problem pronouncing the name of their school.

6. Samira's teacher is dictating some sentences to her class. Samira wants to hear the sentences again.

7. Jian has a doctor's appointment after school. He's having problems reading the bus schedule. He needs someone to show him how to read the schedule.

8. Sam wants to find a bus route on the Internet. He wants his teacher to help him find the route.

9. Grant is working with a volunteer in a group. He can't understand the volunteer. He's speaking too fast. Other students want him to slow down too.

 page 2 Do WB 3. Asking Questions in the ESL Classroom

 Asking Questions in the ESL Classroom

PRONUNCIATION POINTER

INTONATION: THE PITCH DIRECTION OF QUESTIONS

Intonation is the music or song of speaking. Intonation is very important. It tells the listener a lot about what you mean.

PART A

➤ Listen to the following questions that can be answered *yes* or *no*.

➤ Does the voice go up or down at the end of these questions?

1. Can you repeat that, please? ↗

2. Can you explain that, please? ↗

3. Can you help me, please? ↗

4. Can you speak slowly, please? ↗

5. May I borrow an eraser, please? ↗

➤ Listen to each sentence again. Repeat each sentence two times using the correct intonation.

Pronunciation Hint 👄

If you speak without using a range of pitch, other people may think that you are uninterested or unfriendly.

PART B

➤ Now listen to questions that begin with a question word.

➤ Does the pitch go up or down at the end of the questions?

1. What does *level* mean?

2. How do you pronounce this word?

3. How do you spell this word?

4. When is the coffee break?

5. Who is your teacher?

➤ Listen to each sentence again. Repeat each sentence two times, modelling the correct intonation.

General rules for common types of questions in English

Questions that can be answered *yes* or *no*	→	The pitch rises.
Questions that ask for information with a question word: ***What, When, Where, Who***	→	The pitch rises and then falls.

Culture Note

*Use **can** to ask permission in most everyday situations. **May** is used more formally in North America.*

YOUR TURN

➤ Think of other questions beginning with ***can*** or ***may***.

➤ Then think of other questions beginning with **question words**.

➤ Practise saying them to the class following the model above.

Pitch Direction in Questions

FOCUS ON GRAMMAR

USING "GOING TO" TO TALK ABOUT FUTURE PLANS

When we talk about a future plan, we use ***going to***. Look at the following situation:

➤ First, think about your new life in Canada.
I need to speak English well to get a job.

➤ Then, make a plan.
*I'm **going to** register for English classes.*

Subject	Be Verb	Going To	Base Verb	Complement
Affirmative				
I	am	going to	speak	English with my neighbours.
We	are	going to	borrow	books with tapes from the library.
Lawrence	is	going to	volunteer	at his children's school.
Negative				
I	am not	going to	sit	next to a student from my country.
We	aren't	going to	translate	every word in a story.
Lawrence	isn't	going to	worry	about making mistakes.
Question				
Are	you	going to	come	to class every day?
Are	they	going to	review	their lessons in their books?
Is	he	going to	speak	English for a short time every day?

You can use ***going to*** when you want to make short-term and long-term goals about your English.

➤ Read each situation.

➤ Think of a plan for the situation. Then use ***going to*** to write about the plan.

➤ Write your sentences in your notebook.

Pronunciation Hint

Going to *is often pronounced as "gonna."*
Never write "gonna."

EXAMPLE: Rosa is a Benchmark 4. She wants to meet some Canadian people. Can you think of a plan for Rosa?
She is going to talk to the parents at her son's baseball games.

1. Hector wants to read story books to his children. He needs to practise his pronunciation. Can you think of a plan for Hector?

2. Jala wants to improve her listening skills. She is interested in the news and current events. Can you think of a plan for Jala?

3. Renier was in business before coming to Canada. He is a Benchmark 8. He wants to talk to someone about getting some help to set up a business. Can you think of a plan for Renier?

4. Lucinda has friendly neighbours. She needs to speak English on weekends. Can you think of a plan for her?

5. Shu Ren was a nurse before immigrating. She wants to work in a hospital again. She wants to speak to someone about some special nursing courses. She thinks she'll have enough English in about two years. Can you think of a plan for Shu Ren?

6. Van has problems asking questions. It's difficult for her. Can you think of a plan for her?

7. Raquel's teenagers watch movies every weekend. She enjoys watching them with her family, but she needs help to understand what the movie is about. Can you think of a plan for her?

8. Gustavo managed a coffee shop in his community. He wants to get a part-time job while he is studying ESL in the evenings. Can you think of a plan for Gustavo?

YOUR TURN

➤ Think about your short-term and long-term goals.
   What are you going to do?

 page 4 Do WB 4. Using "Going to" for Future Plans

 Using "Going to" for Future Plans

A Letter from the Teacher

Teachers sometimes give students a short information letter about the class.

➤ Read the letter that Bonnie Rogers gave her students.

➤ Can you read and understand the information in the letter?

> Dear Students,
>
> Welcome to our Benchmark Level 3 class. My name is Bonnie Rogers and I will be your teacher. Please call me Bonnie.
>
> Our class starts at 9:30 and ends at 2:30. Please phone the school office when you can't come to school. Phone 779-0416 and leave a message with the secretary. Tell the secretary your name and your teacher's name. Also, say why you are absent.
>
> In our class, we are going to practise listening, speaking, reading and writing. We are going to practise the language that you need every day at work, at school and in the community.
>
> Please come and talk to me if you have any problems. I will also be happy to hear your ideas for our class.
>
> I hope you enjoy our time together.
>
> Sincerely,
>
> Bonnie

Talking It Over

➤ Discuss these questions with a partner.

1. What do you think about a class letter from the teacher? Is it a good idea? Say why or why not.

2. What other information should the teacher put in the letter?

3. Did you receive a letter from your teacher? Did it help you?

 page 5 Do WB 5. Reading a Letter from the Teacher

A Student Application Form

READING 2
WRITING

When you register for a class, you usually have to fill in an application form.

➤ Look at the application form that Parvin filled in.

GLOBAL ADULT ESL CENTRE OF SASKATOON
STUDENT APPLICATION FORM

Student #: ___987654___   Application Date: ___Sept. 16, 2005___

PERSONAL INFORMATION

Please Print
Last Name ___Singh___   First Name ___Parvin___

Address _____212 Cardinal Crescent_____
                        Street and Number

___Saskatoon___   ___Saskatchewan___   ___S7K 2M1___
     City   Province   Postal Code

Home Phone ___(306) 543-1234___   Birth Date ___24/07/76___
                                                 day/month/year

Male ☐   Female ☑

Please answer the following questions:

1. What country are you from?   ___India___

2. What's your native language?   ___Punjabi___

3. When did you arrive in Canada?   ___May 15, 2004___

4. What is your status in Canada?   ___Landed Immigrant___

5. Did you study English in your country?   ___Yes___   How long? ___1 year___

6. Have you studied English in Canada?   ___No___   How long? _____

7. What was your previous job?   ___Seamstress___

8. What is your job in Canada?   ___Hotel Housekeeper___

Medical Number ___888777___   Doctor's Name ___Dr. George Klassen___

Doctor's Phone # ___(306) 498-7654___

Do you have any serious medical problems? ☐   Please list: ___N/A___

If you get sick, who can we phone? Does this person speak English? ___Yes___

Last Name ___Singh___   First Name ___Pal___

Phone ___(306) 499-4323___   Relationship ___Husband___

Date: ___September 16, 2005___   Student Signature: ___Parvin Singh___

OFFICE USE ONLY:	CLB Date 24/08/05	CLB: L3 S3 R3 W2		
Date	**Teacher**	**Location**	**Time**	**Level**
Sept 17/05	John	Global C Rm 5	7:30–9:30	3

Writing Information in the Application Form

➤ Use Parvin's form to complete the paragraph below.

➤ Think about the missing information about Parvin.

➤ Write the paragraph into your notebook.

Parvin filled out her application form on ▭▭▭▭. Her student number is ▭▭▭▭. The name of her school is ▭▭▭▭. She lives in ▭▭▭▭, Saskatchewan. She is from ▭▭▭▭ and her native language is ▭▭▭▭. Parvin has studied English for ▭▭▭▭ year. She works as a ▭▭▭▭ now. If Parvin gets sick, the school can phone Mr. ▭▭▭▭ at ▭▭▭▭. Parvin is in a Level ▭▭▭▭ class. She attends classes every evening from ▭▭▭▭ to ▭▭▭▭. Her teacher's name is ▭▭▭▭.

YOUR TURN

➤ Rewrite the paragraph with information about you. ⟫⟫⟫

📖 **page 6** Do WB 6. Filling in a Student Application Form

Strategies to Help You Learn English   W₁₂ᵣ₃ | WORD PLAY

Do you have some special ways to learn English? Do you like to repeat things out loud? Do you like to write new words in your notebook? It's important for the teacher to know how you like to learn.

➤ Read the list of strategies below. Which strategies do you use? How do these strategies help you?

➤ Next, work with a partner. Make a *yes/no* question about each strategy.

> EXAMPLE: Student A: *Do you like to write down new words*
> *in your notebook?*
> Student B: *Yes, I do. / No, I don't. / Sometimes.*

➤ Write three of your favourite strategies in your notebook.

➤ Find out which strategies are popular with the whole class.

Strategies

1. I like to **write down** new words in my notebook.
2. I like to **guess** the meaning of a word.
3. I like to learn from my **mistakes**. I don't worry about making mistakes.
4. I like to look for the small word or the **base word** in a bigger word. It helps me learn more words.
   Example: *employ, employer, employment, unemployed*
5. I like to talk with students and volunteers in groups. **Discussing** what we are learning helps me a lot.
6. I **practise** English **outside** of the class.
7. I **read over** my exercises. I **review** my lessons at home.

Maybe it means ...

It might mean ...

Cont'd

8. I like to **ask questions**. It helps me to understand.
9. I like to **practise expressions** that I hear a lot.
10. I like to learn the **grammar rules**.

 page 7 Do WB 7. A Survey: Strategies to Help You Learn English
page 8 Do WB 8. Using the Strategy Words

 Classroom Strategies

Communicating in the Classroom  BREAKING IT DOWN

A student in a classroom will use language to do many things. Look at the actions and language functions in the chart. You can use functions like these. They will help you communicate with your teacher and your classmates.

Action	→ Language Function
We tell someone that we don't understand.	Indicating problems in communication
We talk about what we want to do in the future.	Expressing future plans
We talk about how we learn something.	Describing a personal learning routine

➤ Look at the sentences below. Think about what the speaker is doing.

➤ What is the function of each sentence?

➤ Look at the list of three functions. Match each sentence to the correct function.

➤ Write your answers in your notebook.

EXAMPLE: *1. a*

We say

1. Can you please repeat that?

2. Every day, I review my lessons at home.

3. I'm going to finish Level 3 this year.

4. Can you explain that again, please?

5. After I finish ESL classes, I'm going to take a training course.

6. I always write down new words in my notebook.

Learning Strategy

*Learning a second language is different from learning your first language. When you learn a second language, it's helpful to think about what the language is doing. These are called **language functions**.*

Language Functions

a) Indicating problems in communication
b) Expressing future plans
c) Describing a personal learning routine

YOUR TURN

➤ Work in a group. Think of different ways to say that you don't understand.

➤ Use *going to* to talk about your future plans.

➤ Describe your personal learning routine.

➤ Share your group's ideas with the class.

Language in the Classroom

➤ Work with a partner. Practise the kind of language that you might use as a student.

➤ Share your answers with the whole group.

➤ Ask your teacher to make a recording or a video so that you can assess your language.

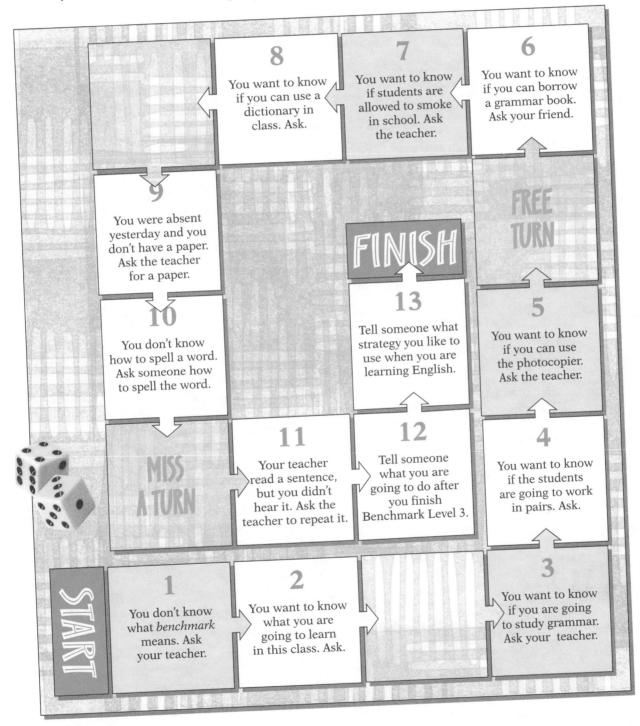

8
You want to know if you can use a dictionary in class. Ask.

7
You want to know if students are allowed to smoke in school. Ask the teacher.

6
You want to know if you can borrow a grammar book. Ask your friend.

9
You were absent yesterday and you don't have a paper. Ask the teacher for a paper.

FREE TURN

FINISH

13
Tell someone what strategy you like to use when you are learning English.

5
You want to know if you can use the photocopier. Ask the teacher.

10
You don't know how to spell a word. Ask someone how to spell the word.

11
Your teacher read a sentence, but you didn't hear it. Ask the teacher to repeat it.

12
Tell someone what you are going to do after you finish Benchmark Level 3.

4
You want to know if the students are going to work in pairs. Ask.

MISS A TURN

START

1
You don't know what *benchmark* means. Ask your teacher.

2
You want to know what you are going to learn in this class. Ask.

3
You want to know if you are going to study grammar. Ask your teacher.

 page 10 Do WB 9. Word Bank
page 11 Do WB 10. Learning Progress Check

At the Library

Learning Opportunities

Do you have the language skills that you need to use the library? Can you ask the librarian for assistance? Do you know how to read directions and renew a book over the phone? Can you read a floor plan or fill in an application for a library card? In this unit, you will learn:

- To ask for assistance.
- To accept assistance.
- To give directions.
- To follow directions.
- To ask for an explanation.
- To read and follow instructions.
- To read a floor plan.
- To fill in a form.

1 – library books 2 – photocopy machine 3 – elevator 4 – librarian

SETTING THE SCENE

When you use the library, you need to know how to talk to the staff at the library. Sometimes, you will want to ask the librarian for assistance. You might need someone to explain how to operate a computer or a photocopy machine. The librarian may give you directions and information. If you want a library card, sometimes you have to fill in a form.

Culture Note

Some public libraries have ESL sections. You can borrow materials to help you learn English.

TALKING IT OVER

1. Describe what you see in the picture.
2. What kind of services does this library have?
3. What do you think the two women will do at the library?

HOW ABOUT YOU?

1. Do you use the library?
2. Do you have a library card?
3. Did you use the library in your community?
4. Compare libraries in your community with libraries in Canada.

WORDS TO THINK ABOUT

1. services
2. story time
3. library books
4. reference
5. photocopy machine
6. elevator
7. to check out
8. library
9. librarian
10. library card
11. computer

 Building Vocabulary

Visiting the Library

 LISTENING

Listening for Key Information

➤ Listen carefully to the conversation between Amina and her friend, Hala.

➤ Your teacher will play the dialogue in parts.

➤ Can you hear the *chunks of language* listed below?

➤ While listening, touch each chunk of language as you hear it. Notice how you can hear the new and important information by listening for the stress. The **stressed words** will be **longer, louder and slower** than the other words.

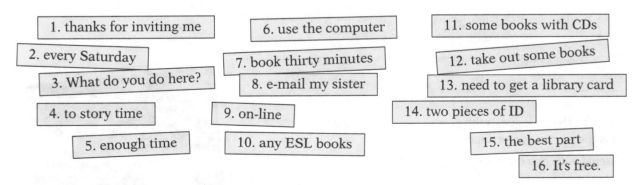

1. thanks for inviting me
2. every Saturday
3. What do you do here?
4. to story time
5. enough time
6. use the computer
7. book thirty minutes
8. e-mail my sister
9. on-line
10. any ESL books
11. some books with CDs
12. take out some books
13. need to get a library card
14. two pieces of ID
15. the best part
16. It's free.

📖 **page 12** Do WB 1. Listening for Key Information

Cont'd

Listening for Details

➤ Read the following questions. Think about what information you need to answer each question.

➤ Listen to the dialogue. Number from 1 to 8 in your notebook. Write down one or two words to answer each question.

➤ Discuss your answers.

1. What does Hala usually do on the weekends?

2. How often does Amina go to the library?

3. Where does Amina take the kids?

4. Does Amina book a computer?

5. What does she do on the computer?

6. Where is the ESL section?

7. What does Hala need to show to get her library card?

8. How much does a library card cost?

YOUR TURN

➤ Work with a partner.

➤ Using the picture on page 16, practise asking each other the questions above.

➤ Answer the questions with a couple of words or a phrase.

EXAMPLE: Student A: *"How often does Amina go to the library?"*
            Student B: *"Every Saturday."*

Listening for the Gist

Getting Assistance

When we use library services and programs, we often need to ***ask for assistance.*** We ask people to help us. When people assist us, they often ***give us directions.*** We need to listen carefully to understand the directions.

Learning Strategy

Watch for body language. It helps you understand when you hear directions.

Excuse me. Can you tell me where the library is?	→	Asking for assistance
Certainly. It's down the street beside the bank.	→	Giving directions

➤ Listen to the dialogue. Is the person asking for assistance or is the person giving directions?

➤ Discuss your choices with your classmates.

page 13 Do WB 2. Getting Assistance

MAKING A POLITE REQUEST

Information ↓   New Card Applications ↓   Returns ↓

There are different ways to ask someone for something in everyday life.

We can say

I would like to reserve a book, please.
OR *I'd like to reserve a book, please.*

I would like to
I'd like to } + base verb

This means you want to reserve a book **now** or **in the future.**

➤ Student A will look at the chart below and make a polite request. Use "I would like to ..." or "I'd like to ..."

➤ Student B will choose a correct response.

➤ Write your answers in your notebook and practise the dialogues.

EXAMPLE: Student A: *"I'd like to apply for a library card, please."*
           Student B: *"Certainly. I'll need to see two pieces of ID*
                        with your address on it."

I'd like to ...	Answer	More information
1. book a computer.	Sure.	We have programs for children six and under.
2. replace a lost library card.	Certainly.	You need a valid library card to book a computer.
3. find out about children's programs for my son.	No problem.	There will be a charge of two dollars for a new card.
4. place a hold on a library book.	Yes.	They're on the second floor, in front of the large print books.
5. find the audio book section.	OK.	The library will call you when the book is available.

 page 13 Do WB 3. Making Requests Using "I Would (I'd) Like To ..."

Choosing Library Services

There are many services at the library.

➤ Read the list of library services. Then, read each person's situation.

➤ Decide which service would be helpful for each person.

➤ Discuss your answers with your classmates.

Library Services

a) room rentals	e) large print books
b) ESL materials	f) free Internet access
c) story time for children	g) videos
d) books and materials in other languages	

Which service would you choose?

EXAMPLE: Amina has small children. She wants them to read and enjoy books. She also wants them to meet other children.
c) story time for children

1. Carlos wants to send e-mails to his old friends. He can't afford to buy a computer.

2. Hala is studying English. She wants to do extra work at home. She can't borrow books from her ESL classroom.

3. Angelina's children like to go to movies, but it is very expensive.

4. Slavko's grandmother lives with him. She enjoys reading. She misses reading books in her language.

5. Anton's grandfather reads in English, but his eyesight is very poor.

6. Hyung Soon's women's group wants to have a meeting.

Helpful Hint

To search for your local library on-line, type in your city + public library.
EXAMPLE: St. John's Public Library

BEYOND THE CLASSROOM

➤ Use the Internet or visit your library.

➤ Get information about the services that your library has.

➤ Share the information with your classmates.

 page 14 Do WB 4. Choosing Library Services

LINKING WORDS IN A PHRASE OR SENTENCE

In connected speech, words in a phrase or sentence are usually linked together without a break between them. They move smoothly from one word to the next.

EXAMPLE: *The copy machine isn't working.*

You link a word that **ends with a consonant sound** with **a word that begins with a vowel sound.**

Rule

When a word ends in a consonant sound and the next word begins with a vowel, the final consonant sounds like the beginning consonant of the following word.

Get information   →   get information = ge-tin-for-ma-tion (5 syllables)

PART A

➤ Listen and repeat these phrases.

1. get information
2. work at home
3. books in other languages
4. get a list
5. place a hold

6. transfer a book
7. have a card
8. meet other children
9. return a book
10. find out about

PART B

➤ Listen and decide where you hear the linking.
➤ Then listen and practise saying these sentences using linking.

EXAMPLE: *You can get information from a librarian.*

1. He wants to send e-mails.
2. She came into the library thirty minutes ago.
3. They read and enjoy books.
4. She finds out about the children's programs.
5. She gets a list of books.
6. His eyesight is very poor.
7. She borrows an ESL book.
8. Where is that grammar book?
9. I can't find it.

PART C

➤ Pick a verb from the Word Box to complete each phrase.

➤ Write these phrases in your notebook.

➤ Then practise with your partner saying the phrases using linking. Be sure that you put stress on the important words in the sentence.

EXAMPLE: *Pick out* a book.

1. ████████ a video
2. ████████ a friend
3. ████████ a meeting room
4. ████████ a good CD
5. ████████ a computer

Word Box

rent

pick out

watch

use

meet

🖥 Linking Words

Asking for Assistance

SPEAKING

Public libraries offer different services. The main branch is usually larger and offers more services than your neighbourhood branch.

➤ Work with a partner. Practise the following conversation.

➤ Use the prompts in the suggestion boxes to change the dialogue. Each number in the example dialogue corresponds to a suggestion box.

Ronald:	**Excuse me.** I don't know how to **use the library catalogue.**
Librarian:	Let me explain **how to log on.** First **click on Basic Search.** Then **follow the prompts.**
Ronald:	Thanks a lot. **I appreciate your help.**
Librarian:	You're welcome. **Just let me know if you need any more help.**

EXAMPLE:

Ronald: *Pardon me.* I don't know how to *book a computer*.

Librarian: Let me explain *how to go on-line*. First *fill in the information*.
            Then *press Enter*.

Ronald: Thanks a lot. *I understand*.

Librarian: You're welcome. *Just call me if you need any more help*.

Suggestion Boxes

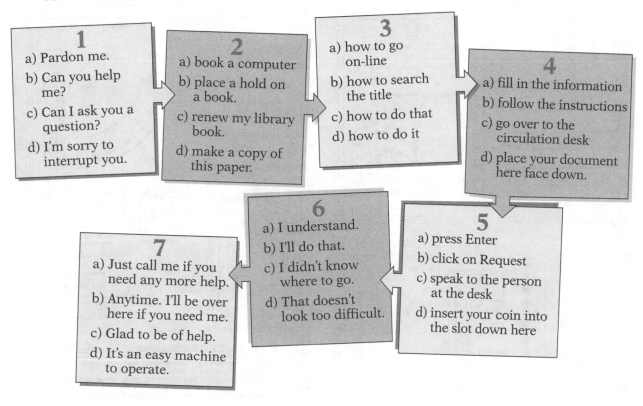

1
a) Pardon me.
b) Can you help me?
c) Can I ask you a question?
d) I'm sorry to interrupt you.

2
a) book a computer
b) place a hold on a book.
c) renew my library book.
d) make a copy of this paper.

3
a) how to go on-line
b) how to search the title
c) how to do that
d) how to do it

4
a) fill in the information
b) follow the instructions
c) go over to the circulation desk
d) place your document here face down.

5
a) press Enter
b) click on Request
c) speak to the person at the desk
d) insert your coin into the slot down here

6
a) I understand.
b) I'll do that.
c) I didn't know where to go.
d) That doesn't look too difficult.

7
a) Just call me if you need any more help.
b) Anytime. I'll be over here if you need me.
c) Glad to be of help.
d) It's an easy machine to operate.

YOUR TURN

➤ Think of services you might need at the library.

➤ Practise asking for assistance. Remember to use polite expressions such as "Pardon me." How would the librarian respond?

➤ Practise the dialogue with a partner.

➤ Present it to the class.

page 15 Do WB 5. Asking Questions about Library Services

 Using Verbs

Using a Map to Give Directions

Here is a floor plan of the Peace Hill Public Library.

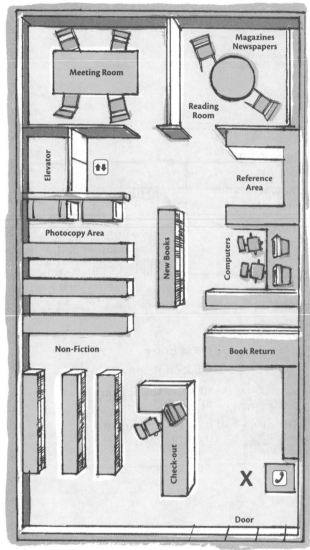

First Floor

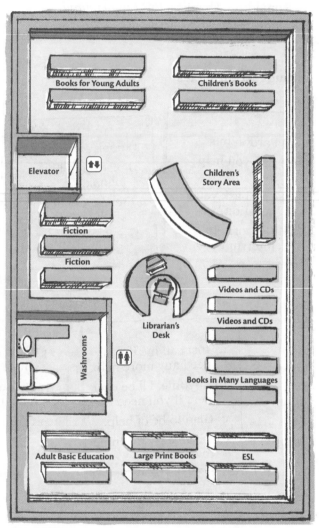

Second Floor

Hala and her friend are at the front door of the library. They want to use the services at the library. How would they ask for directions? What directions would the library staff give them?

➤ Read each question. Then look at the map and give the directions.

➤ Use the choices in the Idea Box.

➤ Work with a partner and practise the dialogues.

EXAMPLE: Hala: Excuse me. Where is the children's story area?

Staff: Take the elevator to the second floor. It's *between the videos and the children's books*.

1. Hala: Pardon me. Where are the computers?
   Staff: They're on the first floor, ________.

2. Hala: Sorry to bother you. How do I get to the ESL section?
   Staff: Take the elevator to the second floor. It's ________.

3. Angelina: Can you help me, please? Where are the videos?
   Staff: Take the elevator to the second floor. They're ________.

4. Dario: Could you help me, please? Do you have any Spanish books?
   Staff: Sure, they're on the second floor, ________.

5. Anton: Excuse me. Do you have books with large print?
   Staff: You can find them on the second floor, ________.

6. Hyung Soon: Pardon me. I'm interested in renting a room for a meeting. Can I see the room?
   Staff: No problem. It's on the main floor, ________.

Idea Box

a) beside the librarian's desk
b) between the videos and the children's books
c) at the back, next to the reading room
d) in the corner, beside the large print books
e) across from the washrooms
f) next to the Adult Basic Education (ABE) books
g) just behind the book return

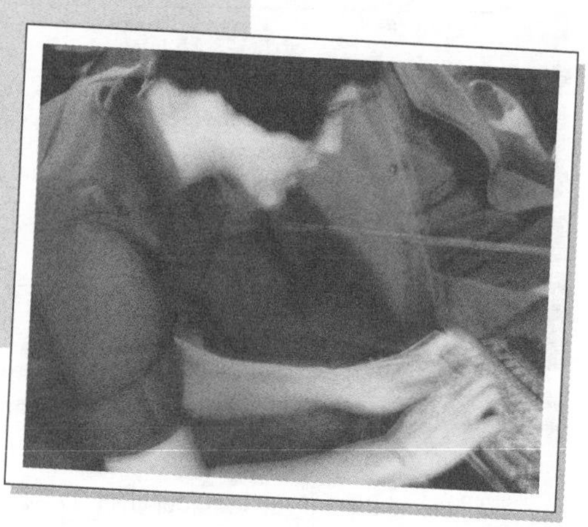

YOUR TURN

- Work with a partner to practise directions. Use the map of the library or your classroom.
- Then write another dialogue asking your own directions.
- Perform one dialogue for the class.

EXAMPLE: Student A: *Where is the public phone?*
Student B: *It's on the main floor, close to the front door.*

page 17 Do WB 6. Following Directions

Reading a Map

Filling in an Application for a Library Card

➤ Read Hala's application for a library card.

➤ Then practise filling in your own application.

PEACE HILL PUBLIC LIBRARY SYSTEM

APPLICATION FOR LIBRARY CARD

Identification with current address is required for applicants 13 years and older

---

(Please print clearly)

Applicant's Last Name _____ Alemayehu _____

First Name _____ Hala _____ Initial(s) _M._

Parent/Legal Guardian (when applicant is under the age of 18)

Last Name _____ N/A _____

First Name _____ Initial(s) _____

Mailing address

_208_ _____ _510_ _____ _Primrose Street_ _____
Apt#   Street#   Street Name

Peace Hill _____ _T8S 1L3_ _____
City   Postal Code

_(780) 775-8866_ _____ _halak@yahoo.com_ _____
Telephone   E-mail Address

Date of Birth _12 / 24 / 75_ _____
m / d / y

Tangerine Industries _____ _5433-100ᵗʰ St._ _____
School/Employer   Address

What is your preferred reading language?

English ☐ French ☐ Other _Amharic_
                            Specify

☐ Please check if you wish your child (12 years or younger)
   to borrow children's materials **ONLY.**

> ### Helpful Hint
> *Dates are written in several ways.*
> *April 15, 2005 can be written 4/15/05, 15/04/05*
> *or 05/15/04. Check for words or abbreviations*
> *to help you: d/m/y.*

STATEMENT OF RESPONSIBILITY: The signer agrees to be responsible for all materials borrowed, and to abide by the rules and regulations of the Peace Hill Public Library. If the signer is under 18, the parent or guardian is responsible for all materials borrowed.

SIGNATURE OF APPLICANT OR PARENT/LEGAL GUARDIAN

Hala Alemayehu   Date _Oct. 21, 2005_

FOR STAFF USE ONLY

Customer Identification # _____   Bar Code # _____

☐ 0-12 XJF   ☐ 13-17 XYF   ☐ 18+ XAF
☐ 0-12 XJM   ☐ 13-17 XYM   ☐ 18+ XAM

Peace Hill Library

1 3079 0 1234567 8

📖 **page 18** Do WB 7. Filling in an Application for a Library Card

Guidelines for Booking a Computer

READING 3

Amina likes to make sure she can use a computer every Saturday.
The librarian gave her a list of guidelines to help her reserve or book
a computer.

➤ Read the guidelines.

➤ Then answer the questions in your notebook.

PEACE HILL PUBLIC LIBRARY

Please follow these guidelines when you reserve a computer. You may book
a computer at any of the branches in the Peace Hill Library System.

1. You need a valid library card and PIN* to book a computer. The PIN
   is the last 4 digits of your telephone number. You can book it on the
   Internet booking system. Click *Booking a Computer.*

2. Only the cardholder can use the computer.

3. You may book a total of 90 minutes per day.

4. You may book a computer four days in advance.

5. Write down the branch, date and time of your computer booking.

6. You MUST log-in within the first ten minutes of your scheduled time
   or your booking will be cancelled.

7. If you see a computer not in use, you may log-in and use it.

8. The computer will automatically log-off when your session expires.

9. If you need help, you may ask the library staff for assistance.

10. Please read our "Computer and Internet Use Policy."

*PIN = Personal Identification Number

Checking for Understanding

1. What do you need to book a computer?

2. Can you reserve a computer using the Internet?

3. Can my friend use a computer that I booked?

4. Can I book a computer for two hours on one day?

5. Can I book a computer one week in advance?

6. How can I remember the date and time for my booking?

7. When must I log-in to use the computer?

8. If no one is using a computer, can I use it?

9. Who can help me with problems using the computer?

10. Should I read and understand the policy for Internet use?

 page 19 Do WB 8. Renewing Your Library Materials

Getting Assistance in the Library

 BREAKING IT DOWN

When you use the library, you will use language to do many things. Look at the language functions in the chart. You can use language functions like these to communicate with people in the library.

Action	→ Language Function
We tell someone that we want them to explain something to us.	Asking for an explanation
We tell someone that we accept their help.	Accepting assistance
We tell someone how to find something.	Giving directions

➤ Look at the sentences below. Think about what the speaker is doing.

➤ Look at the list of three functions that you practised in this unit. Match the sentence with the correct function. Write the answers in your notebook.

EXAMPLE: *1. c*

We say

1. The ESL Section is on the second floor at the back.

2. Thanks for your help.

3. It's on the main floor next to the meeting room.

4. Thank you. I appreciate that.

5. Can you explain how this works?

6. How do I use a library card?

Language Functions

a) Asking for an explanation
b) Accepting assistance
c) Giving directions

YOUR TURN

➤ Work in a group.

➤ Think of different ways to tell someone how to locate something.

➤ Share your group's ideas with the class.

 page 20 Do WB 9. Getting Assistance in the Library

Situations in the Library

➤ Work with a partner.

➤ Practise the kind of language that you might use in the library.

➤ Write what you would say in each situation. When you finish, you will have a dialogue between a librarian and a person using the library.

➤ Practise the dialogue.

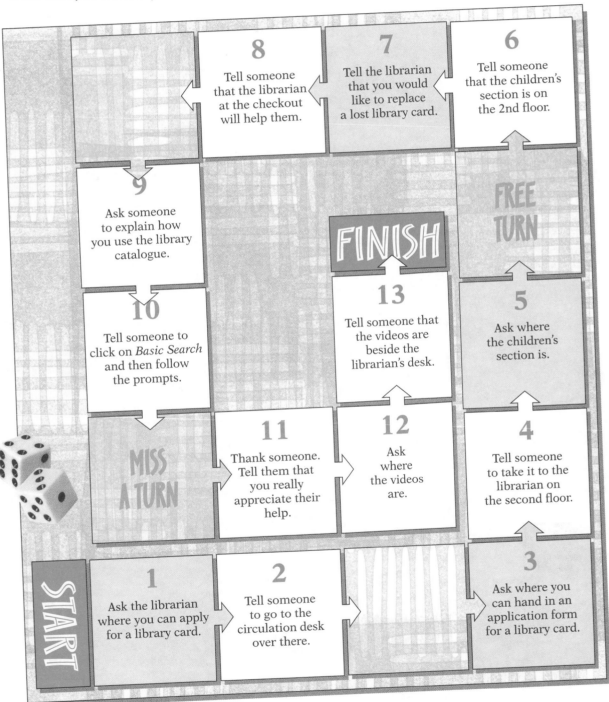

8 Tell someone that the librarian at the checkout will help them.

7 Tell the librarian that you would like to replace a lost library card.

6 Tell someone that the children's section is on the 2nd floor.

9 Ask someone to explain how you use the library catalogue.

FREE TURN

FINISH

13 Tell someone that the videos are beside the librarian's desk.

5 Ask where the children's section is.

10 Tell someone to click on *Basic Search* and then follow the prompts.

MISS A TURN

11 Thank someone. Tell them that you really appreciate their help.

12 Ask where the videos are.

4 Tell someone to take it to the librarian on the second floor.

START

1 Ask the librarian where you can apply for a library card.

2 Tell someone to go to the circulation desk over there.

3 Ask where you can hand in an application form for a library card.

 page 21 Do WB 10. Word Bank
page 22 Do WB 11. Learning Progress Check

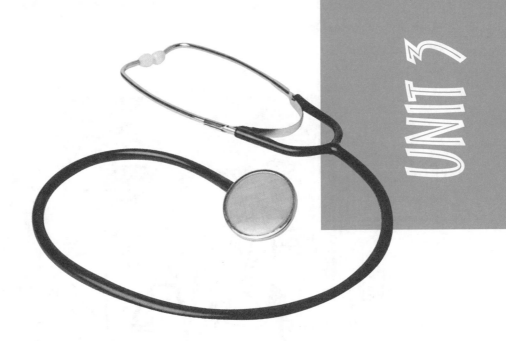

Going to the Doctor

Learning Opportunities

Do you know how to explain your problems to a doctor? Can you understand what your doctor says to you? You may also need to fill in a medical information form and read the instructions on medicine labels. In this unit, you will learn:

- To listen and respond to a doctor's questions.
- How to begin and end a conversation.
- To describe health problems.
- To understand and respond to advice.
- To recognize and use stress and intonation in conversation.
- To read and follow medical directions.
- To fill out a medical history.
- To read a schedule.
- To read a prescription label.

SETTING THE SCENE

When you have a medical problem, you go to the doctor. Patients tell the doctor about their problem. You need to understand the doctor's questions. You may want to ask the doctor for advice. You need to understand the advice you hear. You may have to read and fill out a form.

Culture Note

In North America, people with serious medical problems often wear a special MedicAlert® bracelet. To learn more about the MedicAlert program, visit the website: http://www.medicalert.ca*

* MedicAlert is a Registered Trademark and Service Mark.

TALKING IT OVER

1. Describe what you see in the picture.
2. What do you think is wrong with Malou?
3. What do you think the doctor is saying?
4. What do you think Malou is saying?
5. What do you think the doctor will do?

HOW ABOUT YOU?

1. Some people go to a family doctor when they are sick. Some people go to a clinic or to the emergency room at a hospital. Where do you go?
2. Where have you seen a doctor before?

WORDS TO THINK ABOUT

1. to have a look
2. all over
3. cramps
4. eye infection
5. prescription
6. penicillin
7. antibiotic
8. medical record
9. a reaction
10. MedicAlert
11. rash

A Doctor's Appointment

 LISTENING

Listening for Key Information

➤ Listen carefully to the conversation between Malou and his doctor.

➤ Your teacher will play the dialogue in parts.

➤ Can you hear the *chunks of language* listed below?

➤ While listening, touch each chunk of language as you hear it. Notice how you can hear the new and important information by listening for the stress. The **stressed words** will be **longer, louder and slower** than the other words.

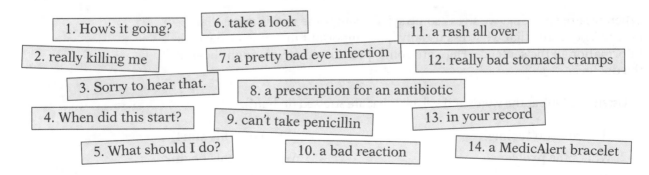

1. How's it going?
2. really killing me
3. Sorry to hear that.
4. When did this start?
5. What should I do?
6. take a look
7. a pretty bad eye infection
8. a prescription for an antibiotic
9. can't take penicillin
10. a bad reaction
11. a rash all over
12. really bad stomach cramps
13. in your record
14. a MedicAlert bracelet

 page 23 Do WB 1. Listening for Key Information

Cont'd

Listening for Details

➤ Read the following questions. Think about what information you need to answer each question.

➤ Listen to the dialogue. Number from 1 to 8 in your notebook. Write down one or two words to answer each question.

➤ Discuss your answers.

1. What is Malou's problem?

2. When did the problem start?

3. What was the doctor's advice?

4. What is Malou worried about?

5. What happened to him before?

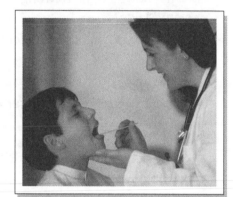

> **Learning Strategy** ♟
>
> *Listen for question words such as:* Who, What, When, *etc. Ask yourself, "What kind of specific information am I listening for?"*

Listening for the Gist

Opening and Closing a Conversation

When you talk with someone, you have a conversation. Someone will open the conversation and someone will close the conversation.

Hi Malou. How is it going?	→	Opening a conversation
Goodbye for now.	→	Closing a conversation

➤ Listen to the dialogue. You will hear ways to open and close a conversation.

➤ Decide if the person is ending a conversation or starting a conversation.

➤ Discuss your choices with your classmates.

📖 **page 24** Do WB 2. Conversation Openers and Closings

PRONUNCIATION POINTER

LISTENING FOR IMPORTANT WORDS IN A SENTENCE

When we are speaking, we stress some syllables in some words more than others. The words that we stress usually have important meaning or have new information in the sentence. Here are some questions that you might hear at the doctor's.

➤ Listen and look at the words and syllables that are stressed (in **bold**).

1. How are you **feel**ing?

2. What's the **pro**blem?

3. What's **wrong**?

4. What **hap**pened?

5. How's it **go**ing?

6. When did this **start**?

7. When did this be**gin**?

8. What should I **do**?

9. Start it to**day**.

10. That's a pretty bad **eye** infection.

YOUR TURN

➤ Think of other questions the doctor asks you.

   EXAMPLE: *Where does it hurt?*

➤ Write these questions in your notebook.

➤ Say them to yourself. Underline the syllables that are stressed.

 Listening for Important Words

Choosing Medical Services

 WORD PLAY

For problems requiring emergency medical help, go to the emergency room. For problems that are not emergencies, go to your family doctor or walk-in clinic.

➤ Work with a partner or in a small group.

➤ Copy the form below into your notebook.

➤ Choose the best medical service for each problem: family doctor/walk-in clinic or emergency room.

➤ Write problems from the Problems Box under the appropriate medical service.

Family Doctor or Walk-In Clinic	Emergency Room
bad cold	*chest pains*

Problems Box

headache	sore throat	flu shot
rash	difficulty breathing	blow or bad bump on the head
severe burn	stomachache	earache
pregnancy	stressed out	fever
check-up	choking	vaccinations
dizziness	broken arm	
serious bleeding	the flu	

YOUR TURN

➤ Can you think of other medical problems?

➤ Where would you go with each kind of a problem?

Filling in a Medical Form

READING 1

SPEAKING

Clinic
Hours:
9 a.m. - 9 p.m.

On your first visit to the doctor's office, the receptionist may ask you to fill out a personal information form. You may also need to answer some questions about your medical history.

➤ Read Malou's completed form. What documents would help him to fill in this form?

➤ Do you understand all of the vocabulary on this form?

➤ Practise asking about personal information with your partner.

PERSONAL INFORMATION

Name ___Abdul_____Malou_____Mohammed___
           last   first   middle

Date of Birth _____June 3, 1972_____   Gender: male __✔__ female _____

Address __#216-2034_____Carlton Street_____
             number   street

___Winnipeg_____MB_____R4R 7G9___
      city   province   postal code

Phone (home) _____986-5744_____ Phone (work)_____775-9631_____

First Language_____Dinka_____ Country of Origin _____Sudan_____

Medical number/health insurance number ___69387___

- -

MEDICAL HISTORY

Doctor's name and phone number _____Dr. Simpson 896-3453_____

Have you been in hospital before?   Yes__✔__No_____

If yes, why?_____I had a broken arm._____

Are you on any medication?   Yes__✔__No_____

If yes, what is it? _____Beta-blockers_____

Do you have any allergies?   Yes__✔__No_____

If yes, to what? _____Penicillin_____

Next of Kin:

Name _____Alakir Mohammed_____ Phone number _669-7475_

Relationship _____cousin_____

Culture Note

It's a good idea to take your medication with you on your first visit to a new doctor.

page 25 Do WB 3. Asking about Personal Information
page 26 Do WB 4. Filling in Personal Information on a Medical Form

Using the Yellow Pages

Walk-in clinics are a good place to go if:
- your medical problem isn't life threatening.
- you can't wait a few days to see the doctor.

Clinics   **351**

Clinics Cont'd

A–Z Health and Wellness Centre
      11–211 Clark St.......555-7215

Anna Freud Health Centre
      240 Wellington St.......895-8705

Associated Walk-in Clinic
      640-310 George St.......555-6664

Autumn Medical Centre
      103 Autumn St.......792-0933

Biotech Pain Relief Centre
      3C–1325 Fifth Ave.......555-8354

Clinics Cont'd

Charles Family Medical Centre
      3360 Charles Blvd.......555-8888

Concord Foot Clinic
      15–210 Concord Ave.......555-2496

Diagnostic X-Ray Clinic
      1555 Maplewood St.......775-9107

Family Therapy Clinic
      121 Osborne Rd.......555-9494

Grand Dental Clinic
      A–419 Grand Blvd. 555-1133

Clinics Cont'd

Pediatric and Adolescent Clinic
      F–2020 Sherbrooke St.......555-1000

Physiotherapy Clinic
      235 Graham Blvd.......867-1517

Point Hope Family Planning Clinic
      189 Westluke Ave.......555-2360

Redwood Women's Health Clinic
      200 Main St.......555-1900

Richmond Community Clinic
      2ndFl–95 Richmond St.......555-2418

➤ Look in the Yellow Pages.

➤ Look at the guide words at the top of each page. These guide words are in alphabetical order. They will help you find information quickly.

➤ Look under *Clinics*.

➤ Answer the following questions. Write your answers in your notebook.

1. How many walk-in clinics are there in your area?

2. Can you find a clinic that is open twenty-four hours a day, seven days a week?

3. Which walk-in clinic is nearest your home?

Learning Strategy

When you are reading the Yellow Pages or a dictionary, guide words *tell what words are on the page. The words are listed in alphabetical order.*

BEYOND THE CLASSROOM

PART A

➤ Phone or visit a walk-in clinic.

➤ Ask the following questions. Write the answers in your notebook.

➤ Share the information with your classmates.

1. What time is your walk-in clinic open?

2. What time do you close?

3. Are you open on weekends?

4. Are you open on holidays?

Cont'd

PART B

Use a copy of a map of your area to plan the route from your home
to the clinic.

➤ Find your home. Put an *H* on it.

➤ Find the nearest clinic. Put a *C* on it.

➤ Plan and highlight the route from your home to the clinic.

➤ Now explain the route to your partner.

FOCUS ON GRAMMAR

USING THE PAST CONTINUOUS TENSE
TO DESCRIBE A PROBLEM

When we go to the doctor, we need to describe a medical problem. We often use
the past continuous verb tense and the simple past to describe the problem.

*I **was walking** to the store when I **fell** on the ice.*

Past Continuous Tense		Simple Past Tense
I was You were He was She was } **walking**	when	I you he she } **fell**
We were They were		we they

In the following conversation, a patient describes a medical problem.

Doctor: What's the matter?

Patient: The other day I was **eating** when I got **stomach cramps.**

➤ Use the above conversation as a model.

➤ Use the Idea Box to write new conversations in your notebook.

EXAMPLE: The other day I was ▓▓▓▓ when I got ▓▓▓▓.

Doctor: What's the matter?

Patient: The other day I was *running*
        when I got *a sore knee.*

Culture Note

*When your doctor explains things to you,
it is okay to ask lots of questions.
EXAMPLES: "Why do I need this medicine?"
"Are there any side effects?"*

Idea Box

Verb	Problem
1. sleep	a nosebleed
2. turn around	dizzy
3. eat ice cream	a toothache
4. jog	chest pains
5. move furniture	a sore neck

Giving Advice Using Should

SPEAKING

After describing a medical problem to a doctor, we usually receive advice. Use **should + base verb.**

    EXAMPLE: *He **should see** a specialist.*

➤ Continue the conversation from the previous activity, page 38.

➤ Use the Idea Box to make new conversations.

    EXAMPLE: Doctor: What's the matter?
                    Patient: The other day I was *running* when I got a *sore knee*.
                    Doctor: You should *see a specialist*.

Idea Box

Verb	Problem	Advice
1. sleep	a nosebleed	get a humidifier
2. turn around	dizzy	keep track of when it happens
3. eat ice cream	a toothache	see your dentist
4. jog	chest pains	have an EKG*
5. move furniture	a sore neck	get an x-ray

*EKG means electrocardiogram. This is a special test to check your heart.

YOUR TURN

➤ Think about other health problems you have had.

➤ What advice did you receive from the doctor?

➤ Share these ideas with your classmates. This is a good way to learn about new remedies.

 page 27 Do WB 5. Giving Advice Using Should

Understanding What the Doctor Says

Using Adjectives to Describe Pain

When we talk about pain to other people or to a doctor, we often use *adjectives* to describe the degree of pain. *Adjectives* help others understand how we feel.

Doctors and nurses sometimes ask you to use a scale to help you describe your pain.

I have a throbbing headache.

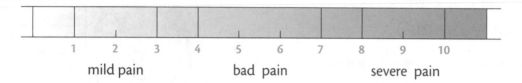

| 1 | 2 | 3 | 4 | 5 | 6 | 7 | 8 | 9 | 10 |

mild pain   bad pain   severe pain

You can describe a headache in different ways.

*I have a **mild** headache.*

*I have a **bad** headache.*

*I have a **severe** headache.*

Headache Pain		
Mild Pain	**Bad Pain**	**Severe Pain**
mild	awful	blinding
dull	terrible	pounding
slight	sinus	throbbing
		splitting

*When you have a **mild** headache, you **should** not take any medicine.*

*When you have a **bad** headache, you **should** take a tablet.*

*When you have a **severe** headache, you **should** go home to bed or see a doctor.*

➤ Practise the sentence below using different adjectives. After the word ***should***, give some advice about headaches.

➤ Write three more sentences in your notebook following the model.

➤ Read your sentences with a partner.

EXAMPLE: When you have a �▮ headache, you should ▮▮▮▮.
When you have a *slight* headache, you should *drink some water*.

A Prescription Label

READING 3

Amoxicillin is a penicillin-like antibiotic. It's used to treat certain infections caused by bacteria, such as ear, lung, nose and skin infections.

➤ Can you read the label?

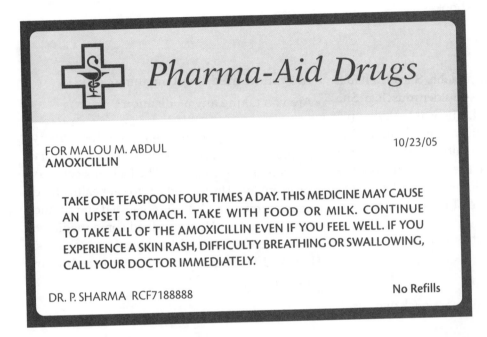

Pharma-Aid Drugs

FOR MALOU M. ABDUL   10/23/05
AMOXICILLIN

TAKE ONE TEASPOON FOUR TIMES A DAY. THIS MEDICINE MAY CAUSE AN UPSET STOMACH. TAKE WITH FOOD OR MILK. CONTINUE TO TAKE ALL OF THE AMOXICILLIN EVEN IF YOU FEEL WELL. IF YOU EXPERIENCE A SKIN RASH, DIFFICULTY BREATHING OR SWALLOWING, CALL YOUR DOCTOR IMMEDIATELY.

DR. P. SHARMA RCF7188888   **No Refills**

➤ Decide whether the following sentences are *true* or *false*.
➤ In your notebook, write *T* for true and *F* for false.

EXAMPLE: *1. T*

1. Amoxicillin is used to treat infections.
2. Take one tablespoon four times a day.
3. This medicine may make you feel sick to your stomach.
4. Take this medicine with water.
5. If you experience difficulty breathing or swallowing, call your doctor.
6. You can stop taking this medicine when you feel well.
7. You can get more of this medicine if you need it.

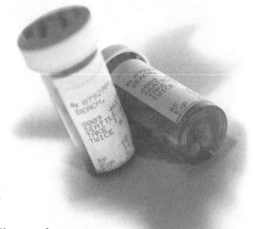

Culture Note

In some provinces in Canada, there is a fee for filling a prescription. It is called a dispensing fee. Ask the pharmacist, "How much is your dispensing fee?"

Reading Prescription Labels

Freshta Finds out about Stress

Freshta is from Afghanistan. She has lived in Canada for two months. This story is about Freshta's health concerns.

➤ Read the story.

➤ Do the activity in your workbook.

Freshta had a terrible headache. She also had a very sore neck and tight shoulder muscles. She wasn't sleeping very well. She was waking up a couple of times every night. She thought that she might have a serious health problem. Freshta decided to see her doctor. Freshta got an appointment right away. Her doctor asked her many questions. Here are some of the questions.

• When did your headaches start?

• Where is the pain?

• Is it a sharp or dull pain?

• How often do you have a sore neck and shoulders?

• Can you get back to sleep?

• Are you worried about anything?

• Are you taking any medication?

Her doctor explained that she had many symptoms of stress. Moving to a new country was causing her to worry. The lack of sleep was a problem too. He advised her to eat healthy food and get more exercise. He suggested she should see a counsellor. He prescribed some medicine for her headaches and her sleeping problems. He asked Freshta to come back to see him in a month.

Feel Empowered

When you can't wait to see the doctor, call the receptionist and say, "I need to see the doctor right away."

Checking for Understanding

➤ Can you make questions about Freshta's story?

 page 28 Do WB 6. Making Questions

 Questions and Answers in the Doctor's Office

Describing Your Symptoms

How do patients describe symptoms?

➤ Work with a partner. Finish the sentences.

Patient

1. I have a ...
2. It's a steady pain ...
3. My shoulders feel ...
4. I wake up ...
5. Sometimes I can't ...
6. I start to ...

a) get back to sleep
b) in the middle of the night
c) worry about my family
d) at the back of my head
e) terrible headache
f) very sore and tight

How do doctors give advice?

➤ Work with a partner. Finish the sentences.

Doctor

1. Talking over your ...
2. Daily exercise ...
3. This medicine will ...
4. Come back to ...

a) relieves stress
b) see me in a month
c) problems with a counsellor can help
d) help you sleep better

 page 29 Do WB 7. Describing Your Symptoms

Hillcrest Park Recreation Centre Schedule

 READING 5

Moving to a new country and learning a new language can be very stressful. Freshta's doctor told her that she should look for fitness classes to help relieve her stress. The Hillcrest Park Recreation Centre is only two kilometres from her home. Freshta works Mondays, Wednesdays and Fridays from 9:00 to 5:00.

➤ Read the following schedule (page 44) and discuss these questions in a small group.

1. Which fitness classes can she attend? When are they?
2. Which classes might help her to relax?
3. Which classes are for older adults?
4. Can she go to a class on Friday evenings?
5. Are there swimming lessons listed in this schedule?
6. Which classes are for muscle building?

Cont'd

7. Freshta wants to attend a fitness class with her neighbour. They are free on Wednesday evenings. Which class should she choose?

8. Freshta would like to go to three classes a week for three months. What is the cheapest way to pay for this? What is the most expensive option?

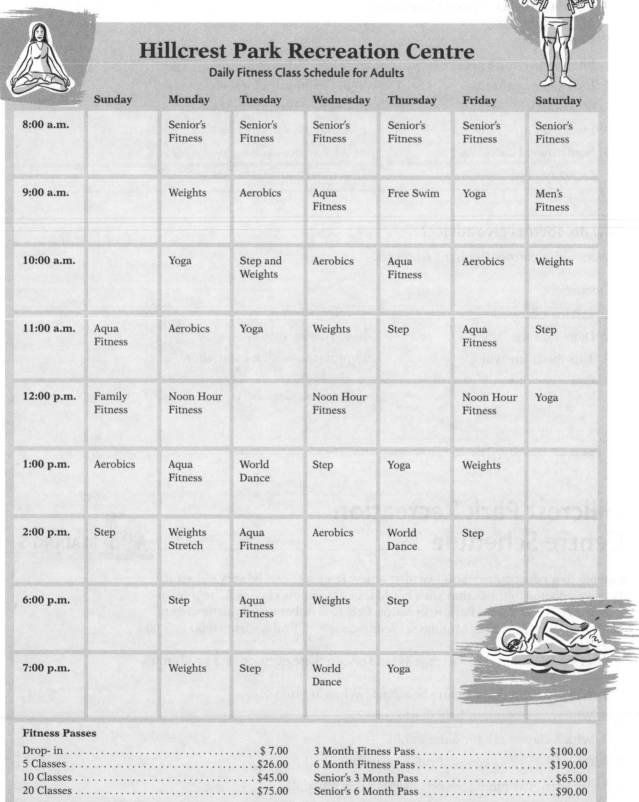

Hillcrest Park Recreation Centre

Daily Fitness Class Schedule for Adults

	Sunday	Monday	Tuesday	Wednesday	Thursday	Friday	Saturday
8:00 a.m.		Senior's Fitness	Senior's Fitness	Senior's Fitness	Senior's Fitness	Senior's Fitness	Senior's Fitness
9:00 a.m.		Weights	Aerobics	Aqua Fitness	Free Swim	Yoga	Men's Fitness
10:00 a.m.		Yoga	Step and Weights	Aerobics	Aqua Fitness	Aerobics	Weights
11:00 a.m.	Aqua Fitness	Aerobics	Yoga	Weights	Step	Aqua Fitness	Step
12:00 p.m.	Family Fitness	Noon Hour Fitness		Noon Hour Fitness		Noon Hour Fitness	Yoga
1:00 p.m.	Aerobics	Aqua Fitness	World Dance	Step	Yoga	Weights	
2:00 p.m.	Step	Weights Stretch	Aqua Fitness	Aerobics	World Dance	Step	
6:00 p.m.		Step	Aqua Fitness	Weights	Step		
7:00 p.m.		Weights	Step	World Dance	Yoga		

Fitness Passes

Drop- in . . . . $ 7.00	3 Month Fitness Pass $100.00
5 Classes $26.00	6 Month Fitness Pass $190.00
10 Classes $45.00	Senior's 3 Month Pass $65.00
20 Classes $75.00	Senior's 6 Month Pass $90.00

YOUR TURN

➤ What do you do for exercise? How often do you exercise?

➤ What fitness centres are near your home? Look in the Yellow Pages to find a centre in your neighbourhood. Find a schedule of fitness classes or fitness leisure activities available in your area.

➤ How much language do you think you need to go to exercise classes?

Language in a Doctor's Office

BREAKING IT DOWN

We use language to do many things. Language has many functions.

➤ Read the following sentences from the conversation between a patient and the doctor.

➤ Match the sentences to their language functions. Write the answers in your notebook.

EXAMPLE: *1. d*

We say

1. Hi Lee. How's it going?

2. My eye is really killing me.

3. How are you?

4. What do you think I should do?

5. My ear is bothering me.

6. You should start it today.

7. When did this start?

8. You should start taking it right away.

9. When did this begin?

10. What should I do?

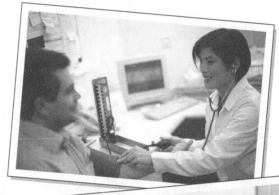

Language Functions

a) Asking for advice

b) Giving advice

c) Describing a problem

d) Greeting or opening a conversation

e) Asking for information

 page 30 Do WB 8. Medical Words to Use

Talking to the Doctor

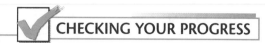 ✓ CHECKING YOUR PROGRESS

➤ Work with a partner to review the language you use when you go to the doctor.

➤ Practise it and then present it to the class.

➤ Do you have the language you need to talk with the doctor?

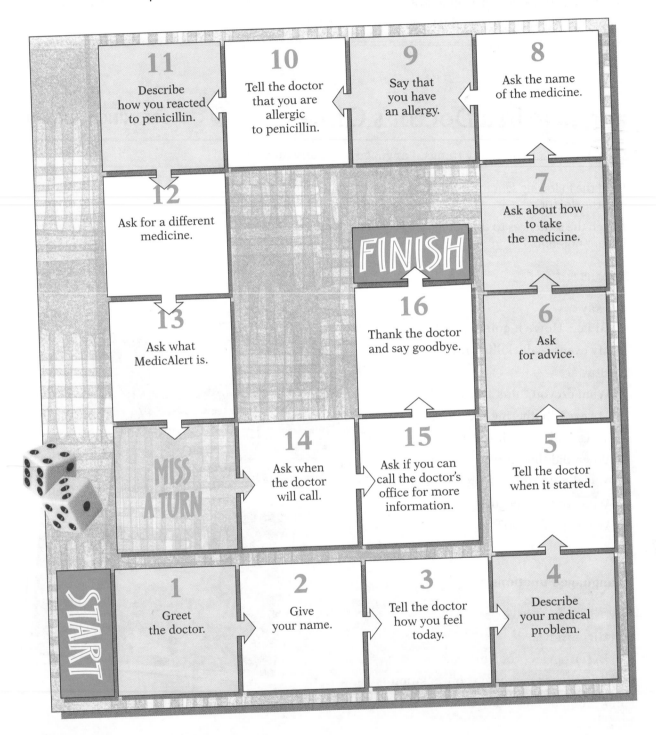

11 Describe how you reacted to penicillin.

10 Tell the doctor that you are allergic to penicillin.

9 Say that you have an allergy.

8 Ask the name of the medicine.

12 Ask for a different medicine.

7 Ask about how to take the medicine.

FINISH

16 Thank the doctor and say goodbye.

13 Ask what MedicAlert is.

6 Ask for advice.

MISS A TURN

14 Ask when the doctor will call.

15 Ask if you can call the doctor's office for more information.

5 Tell the doctor when it started.

START

1 Greet the doctor.

2 Give your name.

3 Tell the doctor how you feel today.

4 Describe your medical problem.

page 31 Do WB 9. Word Bank
page 32 Do WB 10. Learning Progress Check

In the Supermarket

Learning Opportunities

Do you know how to ask for assistance in a store? Can you explain a problem at customer service? Can you read and understand a label on a package? In this unit, you will learn:

- To ask for assistance.
- To follow directions to locate items.
- To ask for clarification.
- To make a request.
- To get information from labels and coupons.
- To fill out a simple form.
- To describe a familiar situation.

1 – clerk 2 – customer 3 – shelf 4 – aisle 5 – sign 6 – point 7 – coupon

"I'm looking for the flour."

SETTING THE SCENE

Before we go shopping, we may read flyers, check coupons and make a list. At the store, we often need to ask for assistance to locate items. We read labels and signs to get information. Sometimes, we fill out application forms to get a discount card to save money.

Culture Note

When we need help in a store, we can ask a clerk or go to Customer Service.

TALKING IT OVER

1. What do you see in the picture?

2. What's the problem?

3. What do you think the customer is saying?

4. What do you think the clerk is saying?

5. What do you think she says when the store employee helps her?

HOW ABOUT YOU?

1. Where do you go shopping?

2. How often do you go shopping?

3. Do you like grocery shopping here?

4. How are stores in Canada different from stores in your community?

WORDS TO THINK ABOUT

1. employee
2. customer
3. shelf
4. aisle
5. sign
6. to point
7. on the right
8. Anything else?
9. whole wheat flour
10. coupon

Save $1.00
Whole Wheat Flour
10 kg on sale!

Going to the Supermarket

LISTENING

Listening for Key Information

➤ Listen carefully to the conversation between Sarah and the store employee.

➤ Your teacher will play the dialogue in parts.

➤ Can you hear the *chunks of language* listed below?

➤ While listening, touch each chunk of language as you hear it. Notice how you can hear the new and important information by listening for the stress. The **stressed words** will be **longer, louder and slower** than the other words.

Helpful Hint

*"Anything else?" means
"Do you want anything else?"*

1. What can I do for you?

2. looking for the flour

3. on sale

4. in the flyer

5. a coupon

6. You mean the 10-kg bag?

7. whole wheat flour

8. That's it.

9. couldn't find it

10. in aisle 5

11. on the bottom shelf

12. all-purpose flour

13. Anything else?

14. Anytime.

Abbreviation note: kg = kilogram

 page 33 Do WB 1. Listening for Key Information

Cont'd

Listening For Details

➤ Read the following questions. Think about what information you need to answer each question.

➤ Listen to the dialogue. Write down one or two words to answer each question in your notebook.

➤ Discuss your answers.

1. Where is Sarah?

2. Who does she ask for help?

3. What does she have a coupon for?

4. Where is the flour located?

5. How does Sarah make sure she understands the directions?

6. Does Sarah receive good service?

Listening for the Gist

Asking for and Giving Directions

When we go to the supermarket, we may need to ask for directions.
Then we have to listen to the person as they give us directions.

Customer: *Where can I find the yogurt?*	→	Asking for directions
Employee: *It's in the back of the store, near the milk.*	→	Giving directions
Customer: *I'm looking for the brown sugar.*	→	Asking for directions
Employee: *Aisle 5. Above the white sugar.*	→	Giving directions

➤ You will hear people asking for directions and giving directions.

➤ Decide if the person is asking for directions or giving directions.

➤ Discuss your choices with your classmates.

Learning Strategy ♟

Listen for question words such as: Who, What, When, *etc. Ask yourself, "What kind of specific information am I listening for?"*

 page 34 Do WB 2. Asking for Directions

What Section Is It In?

Shopping List

Sarah has a shopping list. She only wants to go to a section of the store once. She wants to be organized.

➤ Read the items on the list. Do you understand the meaning of each item?

➤ Work in pairs to decide in which section you would find each item.

➤ Share your answers with the class.

EXAMPLES: Student A: *Where is the shaved ham?*
Student B: *It's in the **deli section.***

Student A: *Where are the oranges?*
Student B: *They're in the **produce section.***

shaved ham	yogurt
lettuce	250g potato salad
2 chickens	broccoli
ground beef	oranges
4 l skim milk	sliced turkey
large coleslaw	lemon cake mix
rye flour	eggs
lemon cake	
cheese slices	
roast beef	
green onions	
lamb chops	
brown sugar	

Abbreviation note: l = litre; g = gram

YOUR TURN

➤ Think of some items you need to shop for.

➤ Write them in your notebook. What section do you think you will find these items in?

🖳 Vocabulary to Use in the Supermarket

there   *who*

PRONUNCIATION POINTER

LIP ROUNDING

For the production of */w/, /oo/, /ow/, /sh/, /ch/, /r/,* and */j/* sounds, the lip position can be described as rounded. Compare your lip position after saying the word **who** and **there**. The sound */oo/* in **who** uses a much more rounded lip position than the */e/* in **there.**

➤ Begin with a warm-up exercise to move the muscles of the mouth. Say: *iy uw iy uw iy uw iy uw.* Your lips are spread when you say the */iy/* sound and rounded when you say the */uw/* sound.

➤ Repeat the underlined words after your teacher.

➤ Then listen to the following questions and repeat after your teacher. Note the roundedness of the lips in the stressed and bolded words.

➤ Work with a partner and practise asking and answering the questions.

Questions

1. Where can I find the **wal**nuts?
2. Where can I find the brown **su**gar?
3. Where can I find the **fro**zen **chi**cken?
4. Where can I find the **fro**zen **shr**imp?
5. Where can I find the **cher**ry pie?
6. Where can I find the **blue**berry **yo**gurt?
7. Where can I find the **fresh straw**berries?
8. Where can I find the **pur**ple **grapes**?
9. Where can I find the **old ched**dar cheese?
10. Where can I find the sliced **tur**key?

Answers

It's	in the	produce section.
They're		dairy section.
		fresh meat section.
		deli.
		baking section.
		grocery section.
		frozen meats.

BEYOND THE CLASSROOM

➤ At home, repeat these questions in front of the mirror.

➤ Do you see the lip rounding?

 Lip Rounding

USING PREPOSITIONS TO LOCATE ITEMS

We use prepositions to describe where something is located. Which preposition should you use? Think about the location. Then choose the preposition.

At

The location is a point or place.

At the grocery store.
At the deli.
At the back.
*The deli is **at** the back of the store.*

To

The location is moving in a direction.

*Come **to** customer service.*
*Go **to** aisle 5.*
*Milk is **to** the right of the juice.*

On

The location is a surface.

***On** the table.*
***On** the floor.*
***On** the shelf.*
*My groceries are **on** the counter.*

In

The location is an area.

***In** a room.*
***In** a box.*
***In** the corner.*
*The flowers are **in** the corner.*

In the supermarket, we often follow a clerk's directions to locate the items that we are looking for.

➤ Look at the picture of the store shelves.

➤ How would a clerk describe the location of items on these shelves?

➤ Complete the sentences below the picture on page 54.

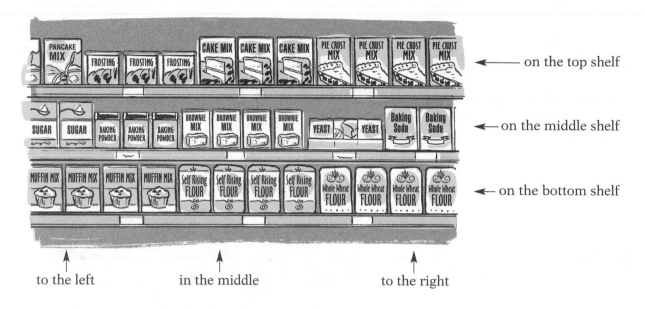

on the top shelf

on the middle shelf

on the bottom shelf

to the left   in the middle   to the right

EXAMPLE: Customer: I'm looking for the whole-wheat flour.
            Clerk: It's *in* aisle 5, *on* the bottom shelf, *to* the right
                         of the self-rising flour.

1. Customer: I can't find the baking powder.
   Clerk: It's ▮▮▮▮ aisle 5, ▮▮▮▮ the middle shelf, ▮▮▮ the left.

2. Customer: Where can I find the cake mixes?
   Clerk: They are ▮▮▮▮ aisle 5, ▮▮▮▮ the top shelf, ▮▮▮ the middle.

3. Customer: Where is the self-rising flour?
   Clerk: It is ▮▮▮▮ aisle 5, ▮▮▮▮ the bottom shelf, ▮▮▮ the middle.

4. Customer: Could you tell me where the yeast is?
   Clerk: You will find it ▮▮▮▮ aisle 5, ▮▮▮▮ the middle shelf,
                ▮▮▮ the right.

5. Customer: I can't seem to find the muffin mix.
   Clerk: Try looking ▮▮▮▮ aisle 5, ▮▮▮▮ the bottom shelf,
                ▮▮▮ the left.

🖥 Putting Items in the Cupboard

Giving and Clarifying Directions

SPEAKING

When Sarah goes shopping, she sometimes can't find what she is looking
for in the store. She has to ask a store clerk for directions. The store clerks are
very helpful, but they speak very quickly. It is difficult for Sarah
to listen and remember. Sarah repeats the important words again. If she
makes a mistake, the clerk will correct her.

➤ Read and role-play the dialogues with a partner.

➤ Student A gives the directions with the book.
   Student B clarifies the directions without the book.

➤ Switch roles and try again.

Learning Strategy ♟

*Repeating what you hear is a listening
strategy. It helps you check what
you hear.*

EXAMPLE:

Student A: *It's in aisle 5.*   Student B: *In aisle 5?*

STUDENT A	**STUDENT B**

STUDENT A

1 You'll find it in the dairy section.

2. It's in aisle 5, second shelf from the top, on the right-hand side.

3. They're in the meat department, between the chicken and the beef.

4. It's in the bakery, on the top shelf.

5. It's at the end of aisle 5, on the middle shelf, between the beans and the macaroni.

6. They're at the back of the store, on the left-hand side, in the corner.

7. They're in the produce section, along the far wall.

8. They are at the end of aisle 7.

9. They are at checkout number 10, next to the magazines.

STUDENT B

1. The dairy section?

2. Aisle 5? Second shelf from the top? On the right?

3. The meat department? Between the chicken and the beef?

4. The bakery? Top shelf?

5. Aisle 5? Middle shelf? Between the beans and macaroni?

6. At the back? Left-hand side? In the corner?

7. The produce section? Along the far wall?

8. Aisle 7? At the end?

9. Checkout 10? Next to the magazines?

Food Labels

READING 1

When you are shopping, it is important to read and understand food labels.

➤ Read these labels. What kind of information do you see?

SAFE FOODS Ltd

Extra Lean Ground Beef

1 kg

| Packaged on | July 10 |
| Best before | July 13 |

LAKESiDE DAiRY

❀

Cottage Cheese 2%

| Best before Jan 19 | Keep refrigerated |

Green Valley

Fresh Farm Eggs

1 dozen

Best before Feb. 9

Best before Feb 3

DRINKALOT

Skim Milk

Vitamins A & D added

Fat Free 0.1% mf

2 litres

Abbreviation note: mf = milkfat

Cont'd

➤ Read the sentences below.

➤ Decide whether the statement is *true* or *false*. Write *T* or *F* in your notebook.

EXAMPLE: Ground beef should be used within three days. *T*

1. This carton of milk is fat free.
2. There are fifteen eggs in this carton.
3. Vitamin A and D are added to the cottage cheese.
4. You should look for a *best before* date when you buy eggs.
5. You should eat the ground beef before July 10.
6. You should refrigerate all of these food items.
7. The milk has vitamins added.
8. The ground beef has fat removed.
9. The eggs come from Lakeside Dairy.
10. You can use the cottage cheese on January 25.

YOUR TURN

➤ Think about the labels on products that you have at home. What do they tell you?

- Name of the product
- Name of the company
- Size or weight of the product
- Kind of product
- Expiry dates
- Information about food handling
- Ingredients/nutritional value

➤ Bring a label from home to show, read and discuss together.

page 34 Do WB 3. Nutrition Labels
page 36 Do WB 4. Unit Price Labels

Filling in a Store Membership Card

READING 2

WRITING

Sometimes you can save money if you have a special card from a store. You need to apply for the card

➤ Read the information about the OK Foods Savings Card and Sarah's completed application.

➤ Use her application as a model to fill in your own savings card application form.

➤ Remember to print neatly with block letters. Use spaces when necessary. Make sure all letters and numbers are legible.

➤ Remember to use only two digits for the month, day and year.

EXAMPLE: 05/10/73

Free Membership!
Sign Up Today!

Fill out the attached application and give it to the cashier at the checkout today. You will receive your OK Foods Savings Card immediately. You will start saving instantly.

- - - - - - ✂- ✂- - - - - - -

OK Foods Savings Card Application

Applicants must be 18 years of age or older to apply for a savings card.

| PLEASE PRINT CLEARLY | Check one: | New Member | ✔ |
| | | Replacement Card | ☐ |

N	A	R	S	O																					

Applicant's Last Name

S	A	R	A	H																A					

First Name   **M.I.**

5	4	3		O	A	K		S	T	R	E	E	T												

Street Address   **Apt#**

W	I	N	N	I	P	E	G								M	B									

City   **Province**

R	3	N	7	B	5																				

Postal Code

0	5		1	0		7	3																		

Birth Date (month/day/year)

7	7	5		0	0	4	8																		

Home Phone

Sarah Narso   04/29/05

Applicant's Signature   **Date**

We respect your privacy. OK Foods does not sell or lease personally identifying information (i.e., your name, address and telephone number) to other companies.

Complete this form and receive your OK Savings Card instantly!

Abbreviation note: M.I. = middle initial; i.e. = that is to say

Culture Note

Giving out your date of birth is usually optional but people give this information to medical or government offices.

 page 37 Do WB 5. Filling Out a Store Membership Card

Asking for Assistance

Sometimes it's difficult to know what to say when you have a problem at the grocery store. You want to ask for help in a polite way.

Often being polite means softening your request. We use modals, questions and intonation to sound more polite. Imperatives can sometimes sound rude.

Would you **Could** you } check this price for me?	→	is more polite than	→	*Check this price for me.*
I think *you made a mistake.*	→	is more polite than	→	*You made a mistake.*
I'm sorry *but I don't want this cake.*	→	is more polite than	→	*I don't want this cake.*
Could *I return this milk? It's sour.*	→	is more polite than	→	*This milk is sour.* *Give me my money back!*
Will *you help me?*	→	is more polite than	→	*You will help me.*

➤ Work with a partner.

➤ Read the following situations (page 59). Two of the answers are better because they are polite. One answer is not polite.

➤ How would you ask for assistance? Talk about your choices.

EXAMPLE: Frieda is at the checkout counter. The cashier charged her the regular price for the chicken, but it is on sale. What do you think Frieda should say?

a) That's wrong. That's not the price.

b) I think there is a mistake. Chicken is on sale this week.

c) Excuse me. There's a mistake. I think you charged me too much.

Answer: *b and c are better than a which is not polite*

1. Slavko bought a birthday cake for his daughter's birthday. When he got home from the store he checked his receipt. He paid for the cake twice. He went to Customer Service with his receipt.

a) I bought a cake. I checked my bill when I got home. I was charged twice for the same cake. Could I please get a refund?

b) Look at this. I was charged twice for the same cake. I want my money back.

c) Would you check my receipt? It looks like I was charged twice for the same item.

2. Martha bought apples at the grocery store last week. When she ate one, it was rotten in the middle. She cut open a few more. They were rotten too. Martha decided to return them to the store. She put the apples in a bag and got her receipt. She went to Customer Service.

a) I bought these apples. They're rotten in the middle. Give me my money back!

b) I'd like to return these apples. I cut open three of them and they're rotten inside. Here is my receipt. I circled the item for you.

c) Here's my receipt. I bought these apples last week and three of them are rotten. I'd like a refund please.

3. David was at the checkout counter. He was watching the cashier scan his groceries. She turned to him and said, "That will be $80.34." David reached into his pocket. He didn't have his wallet.

a) Excuse me. I'm really sorry. I left my wallet at home. I can't pay you. What should I do?

b) Oh, no! I don't have my wallet. I'm going home to get it. You watch my cart.

c) I'm so embarrassed. I don't have my wallet. Can I leave my cart at customer service while I go home for my wallet?

4. When Hector was shopping, he bought a pineapple. When the cashier scanned the price, he changed his mind. He didn't want it. He asked the cashier to take the pineapple off his bill.

a) Oh no! That's too expensive. I hope you don't mind, but I don't want that pineapple. Could you take it off my bill? Sorry.

b) I apologize, but I don't want that pineapple.

c) Oh, that's too expensive. Take it off my bill!

COMPARISONS

In the next reading, you'll see some examples of comparative adjectives.

Rule	Example
If an adjective has one or two syllables, add the suffix *er*. If the adjective ends in *y*, change the *y* to *i* and add *er*.	wide → *wider than* noisy → *noisier than*
If an adjective has more than two syllables, use **more/less** or **fewer** with the comparative adjective.	expensive → **more** *expensive* expensive → **less** *expensive*
To write a negative comparative, write **the negative verb + as + adjective + as.**	|*isn't*| **as** |*fresh*| **as** negative verb adjective

Shopping Experiences in Two Countries READING 3

Read the following stories written by students.

➤ What did they say to start their stories?
➤ How did they use adjectives to compare shopping in their country and Canada?
➤ Write down the comparative adjectives in your notebook.

Shopping for Food in Ethiopia and Canada

There are many differences between shopping for food in Ethiopia and Canada. First, the stores in Canada are much bigger than in my country. When we go shopping in Canada, we drive. The stores have big parking lots in front. In Ethiopia, the stores are closer so we can walk. There are many kinds of small stores. Each one sells something different. One sells fruit and vegetables. Another sells meat. Another sells bread.

In my country, we have to go shopping earlier in the day to get food. The food is fresher than in Canada. We don't eat frozen food there. I feel more comfortable shopping there because I can ask more questions. The stores are not self-serve. The store owner gives the fruit and vegetables to the customers. I pay cash in my country because people don't have credit cards. I like shopping in my country.

Story by Hadish

Food Shopping in Two Countries

In China, shopping is different than in Canada. First, there are many small stores around the city. It's more convenient for people to buy food there. In Canada, the supermarkets are fewer and larger. They are not located in the neighbourhoods where people live. Second, in my hometown, people like to go to the restaurant to eat fresh food. Many people don't like cooking at home. They are very busy and Chinese cooking takes more time. Also, the food there is not as expensive as here.

Finally, in China, the cities are very crowded. The stores are more crowded than in Canada. Some of the people just watch other people buying things. Here, the stores are less crowded and cleaner. The shopping is more enjoyable here.

Story by Tien Long

➤ Look back at the stories again. Note how these students have used different words to describe and compare shopping.

➤ Notice the use of transition words: *first, second, also, finally,* etc.

 page 60 Do WB 6. Making Comparisons

Tips for Grocery Shopping in Canada

 SPEAKING

Grocery shopping is challenging. We want to buy nutritious food for the least amount of money.

➤ Work in groups to read and talk about the questions below.

➤ Share some tips with your group.

➤ Make a list of all the tips with your class.

1. Do you look in your cupboards and fridge to see which items you already have?

2. Do you read the grocery ads to see which items are on sale?

3. Do you write a shopping list?

4. Do you find coupons for the food you need?

5. Do you look carefully at what you are buying, such as:
   • reading the nutrition labels;
   • looking for fruit that is not bruised;
   • looking for vegetables that are not rotten;
   • checking the *best before, expiry,* or *packaged on* dates when you buy items like eggs, milk, cereal, or over the counter medicines?

Cont'd

6. Do you check the unit prices on products to compare prices?

7. Do you buy fruits and vegetable in season?

8. Do you shop at a store where the prices are competitive? Do you shop at a convenience store? Why or why not?

9. Do you watch the cashier as she/he scans your grocery items?

10. Do you check your receipt for mistakes?

Culture Note

You can ask for a raincheck if you can't find an item that is on sale. Using coupons is a good way of saving money.

📖 **page 39** Do WB 7. Read and Understand a Coupon

💻 Reading about Nutritious Snacks

Conversations

 **BREAKING IT DOWN**

Conversations have an order to them. Conversations are made up of sentences. The sentences in conversations are a collection of language functions.

Action	→ Language Function
We begin a conversation.	Opening a conversation
We end a conversation.	Closing a conversation
We ask for help.	Asking for assistance
We say that we will help.	Offering assistance
We tell someone how to do something.	Giving directions
We ask someone to make something clearer.	Asking for clarification

➤ Read the following sentences from a conversation between a grocery clerk and a customer.

➤ Match the sentences to their language functions. Write the answers in your notebook.

EXAMPLE: *1. c*

We say

1. Can you help me?

2. What can I do for you?

3. You mean the 10-kg bag of whole wheat flour?

4. It's in aisle 5 on the bottom shelf.

5. Do you need help with anything else?

6. Thank you very much for your help.

7. Excuse me. Can you help me?

Language Functions

a) Opening a conversation

b) Closing a conversation

c) Asking for assistance

d) Offering assistance

e) Giving directions

f) Asking for clarification

📖 **page 40** Do WB 8. Getting Help at the Store
page 41 Do WB 9. Word Bank

Field Trip to a Supermarket

✓ **CHECKING YOUR PROGRESS**

You are going to visit a supermarket to practise your English. Ask the store clerks to help you if you can't find an item. You will practise your English in the following ways:

- You will ask and listen to directions.
- You will locate items and prices.
- You will follow instructions.
- You will read a map.

➤ Work with your partners to find the answers at the supermarket.

➤ Write your answers in your notebook.

➤ Compare your answers with your classmates.

1. Find the cinnamon.

   a) Which aisle is it in?

   b) What is to the left of the cinnamon?

   c) How are the spices arranged?

2. Find the frozen corn.

   a) What section of the store is it in?

3. Find the washrooms.

   a) Are the men's and women's washrooms next to, or across from each other?

4. Find the laundry detergent. Read the label. Compare a store brand to a name brand of the same size.

   a) How many loads can you wash?

   b) Which detergent is cheaper?

   c) Which detergent washes more loads?

   d) Which detergent washes fewer loads?

5. Look at the beef in the fresh meat department.

   a) What kind of beef is the most expensive per kg?

   b) What is the cheapest per kg?

6. Find an item on sale this week.

   a) If you buy one item, do you pay the sale price or the regular price? Ask a store clerk.

7. Go to the deli. Ask a clerk if you have to pay tax on a roasted chicken.

8. Go to the meat department. Ask a clerk if you have to pay tax on a fresh chicken.

YOUR TURN

➤ Take pictures on the field trip. Use them in the classroom to talk about your experiences.

➤ Write a 5–8 sentence paragraph to describe the experience.

 page 42 Do WB 10. Learning Progress Check

Reporting
a Medical Emergency

Learning Opportunities

Do you know how to save a life, help someone in an emergency and call 9-1-1 for emergency help by using the telephone? When you use the emergency telephone number 9-1-1, you need to deliver a clear message. In this unit, you will learn:

- To request urgent assistance.
- To describe a person or a situation.
- To follow one to five instructions on first aid.
- To find information in a pamphlet and a directory.
- To fill out an identification form for medical emergencies.
- To respond to expressions of caution or warning.
- To follow directions in an emergency.
- To respond to questions from an emergency operator and an emergency admittance clerk.

"We have a medical emergency. A child is having trouble breathing. It's a possible peanut allergy."

SETTING THE SCENE

Sometimes we have to deal with medical emergencies. We need language to report an emergency and describe an injured person or a situation. We have to listen to instructions from an emergency operator. The operator may caution or warn us. Sometimes, we read instructions to keep us safe. If there is an accident at work, we may have to fill out forms.

Culture Note

You don't need to pay to make an emergency call from a pay phone. Just dial "0" and tell the operator that it is an emergency.

TALKING IT OVER

1. Describe what you see in the picture.
2. Who is the principal calling?
3. Why is she calling?
4. What caused the problem?

HOW ABOUT YOU?

1. Have you ever called 9-1-1 in an emergency?
2. What was the emergency?
3. Who came to help you?
4. Did you have to pay for an ambulance?
5. Describe how you would get emergency medical help in your community.

WORDS TO THINK ABOUT

1. possible
2. allergic reaction
3. cross street
4. on the way
5. to direct us
6. epi-pen
7. conscious
8. to swallow
9. swollen

Reporting an Emergency

LISTENING

Listening for Key Information

➤ Listen carefully to the conversation between the caller and the 9-1-1 operator.

➤ Your teacher will play the dialogue in parts.

➤ Can you hear the *chunks of language* listed below?

➤ While listening, touch each chunk of language as you hear it. Notice how you can hear the new and important information by listening for the stress. The **stressed words** will be **longer, louder and slower** than the other words.

Pronunciation Hint

Sometimes words are linked and sound as if they are one word.

1. possible allergic reaction
2. elementary school
3. nearest cross street
4. on the way
5. to direct us
6. epi-pen
7. in his file
8. conscious
9. swallow
10. lips look blue
11. swollen
12. medical number

 page 43 Do WB 1. Listening for Key Information

Cont'd

Listening for Details

➤ Read the following questions. Think about what information you need to answer each question.

➤ Number from 1 to 7 in your notebook.

➤ Listen to the dialogue. Write down one or two words to answer each question.

➤ Discuss your answers.

Culture Note

Some health insurance plans cover ambulance service. Sometimes, we have to pay. For example, you might get a bill for $250.

1. Who speaks first in this dialogue?

2. Is the boy having an allergic reaction?

3. Who is making the 9-1-1 call?

4. Where is the boy?

5. Is the school near Albert Street?

6. Did the principal use an epi-pen?

7. What's wrong with the boy's lips?

YOUR TURN

➤ Work with a partner.

➤ Practise asking each other the questions about the 9-1-1 call.

➤ Answer the questions with a couple of words or a phrase.

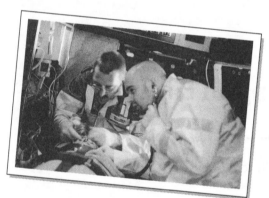

Listening for the Gist

Asking for Information and Giving Instructions

When you call 9-1-1, the emergency operator will ask you for information. The operator will also give you instructions.

What is the nature of the injury? →	Asking for information
Keep the person warm and calm. →	Giving instructions

➤ Listen to the emergency operator.

➤ Decide if the operator is giving instructions or asking for information.

➤ Discuss your choices with your classmates.

 page 44 Do WB 2. Listening to the Emergency Operator

MAJOR SENTENCE STRESS

In English, the major stress in the sentence usually occurs on the word with the **new** or **most important** information. This is often called the *information focus* of a sentence. Major sentence stress in a sentence often falls on the last content word of a sentence. You can hear the stressed word in a sentence because it will be **louder** and **longer**. It will have a **clearer sounding vowel**. It will also have a **change in pitch**.

> EXAMPLES: *The boy just ate some* **peanuts**.
> *Is he* **conscious**?
> *We're just north of* **Albert** *Avenue*.
> *The boy is allergic to* **peanuts**.
> *Is he* **breathing**? *Does he use an* **epi-pen**?

➤ Listen as your teacher models the sentences above. Notice the major stress on the bolded word.

➤ Practise the sentences with a partner.

Pronunciation Hint 👄
- -
Pitch is the music of the language. With a change in pitch, your voice goes up or down. Listen for the pitch when you are speaking.

 page 44 Do WB 3. Major Sentence Stress

 Major Sentence Stress

USING THE PAST TENSE WITH "JUST"

When we call 9-1-1, we have to describe the emergency. We have to tell the operator what happened. Use the simple past tense with the word *just* to explain that something happened very recently.

Subject		Simple Past	Object
The boy	*just*	had	an allergic reaction.
We	*just*	called	9-1-1.
The operator	*just*	sent	the ambulance.

➤ Write the correct form of the verb with *just* to describe something that just happened to Mohammed.

➤ Write the answers in your notebook.

> EXAMPLE: A young boy (just / to eat) *just ate* a peanut butter sandwich.
> He is allergic to peanuts!

1. He (just / to have) ░░░░░░ a severe reaction to peanuts.

2. His teacher (just / to call) ░░░░░░ the principal on the intercom.

3. They (just / to rush) ░░░░░░ the boy to the principal's office.

4. The principal (just / to phone) ░░░░░░ 9-1-1.

5. His teacher (just / to check) ░░░░░░ his file for medical information.

6. The principal (just / to answer) ░░░░░░ questions from the 9-1-1 operators.

7. Someone (just / to go) ░░░░░░ outside to wait for the ambulance.

Reporting Medical Emergencies

SPEAKING

In a conversation with the emergency operator, we have to describe the emergency in order to get the help we need. One of the most important questions you answer is, "Where are you located?"

➤ Read the conversation below between a caller and the 9-1-1 operator.

➤ Work with a partner. Practise describing your location and a medical emergency.

9-1-1 operator:	What are you reporting?
Caller:	My husband just had a heart attack.
9-1-1 operator:	What's your location?
Caller:	I'm at 610 Main Street, apartment number 10.

9-1-1 operator:	What's the nearest cross street?
Caller:	It's Broadway.
9-1-1 operator:	Which door should the ambulance come to?
Caller:	Come to the back door/the side door/the front door.
9-1-1 operator:	The ambulance is on the way.

YOUR TURN

➤ Take turns being the operator and the caller.

➤ Use the following four situations to report a medical emergency.

➤ Try using different addresses, for example, at home, at school, at work, or at your friend's home.

Situations

1. My son just burned himself in the bathtub.

2. My toddler just swallowed some of my medicine.

3. My neighbour just fell down the stairs.

4. A car just hit someone.

Culture Note

If you live in an apartment, say the street address first. Then give the apartment number at the end. EXAMPLE: *My address is 1307 Rose Street, apartment 25.*

Emergency Information in the Telephone Directory

READING 1

It's a good idea to be prepared for an emergency. The telephone directory can help you.

➤ Read the following text carefully.

If you look in the first few pages of your phone directory, you will probably see the numbers **9-1-1** in large bold print. This is the phone number of Emergency Services in many cities and towns in Canada and the United States. It tells you about emergency services and what to do in the case of an emergency.

Emergency Services include fire, ambulance, police and poison treatment. An emergency is:

• any serious medical problem (chest pain, seizure, bleeding);

• any type of fire (business, car, building);

• any life-threatening situation (fights, person with weapons);

• any crime in progress (whether or not a life is threatened).

Cont'd

Follow these steps in an emergency:

1. Call 9-1-1 and ask for the service you need.

2. Give the location of the emergency and the nearest major cross street. In emergencies, help or **first responders** will be sent while you are giving the information to the emergency operator. A *first responder* could be a fire rescue truck, police car or ambulance.

3. Remember that the emergency operator can see the phone number you are calling from on a screen. This helps emergency responders to contact you if you can't complete the call.

4. Give a description of the emergency situation.

5. Answer the emergency operator's questions.

6. Follow the instructions that the person gives you.

7. The ambulance will take the person to the emergency department.

8. The most urgent emergency situation is attended to first. This is called **triage.** If your problem is less serious, you may have to wait.

9. If you don't have a life-threatening situation, call the non-emergency police or health service phone number. Don't call 9-1-1.

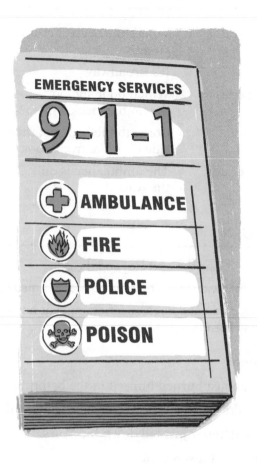

Talking It Over

PART A

➤ Talk about any experiences you have had with emergency services.

➤ Use the questions below in your discussion.

1. Have you ever called for emergency service? When and where?

2. What was the emergency?

3. What questions did the operator ask you?

4. Did the operator give you special instructions? What were they?

5. What did the emergency attendants do?

6. How did you feel? Were you calm or did you panic?

7. What kind of emergencies do you need to learn about?

Culture Note

Use the non-emergency number in your phone book to get information about 9-1-1. Never call 9-1-1 except for emergencies!

PART B

➤ Read the information below. Which of the reasons do you think are appropriate to call 9-1-1?

➤ Discuss them with the class.

Why Do People Call 9-1-1?

One Canadian survey found that people call 9-1-1 for the following reasons: highway conditions; fire; robbery; an accident; sudden illness; a crime; missing person; explosion.

 page 45 Do WB 4. Identify the Emergency Service Needed

YOUR TURN

It's important to have a list of emergency numbers close to the phone. Keep it in a permanent place.

➤ Fill in important emergency numbers for your family. Remember to put this list near your phone at home.

 page 46 Do WB 5. Emergency Phone Numbers

What Medical Emergency Are You Reporting?

WORD PLAY

We need a lot of language to report a medical emergency.

➤ Look at each of the situations where someone calls 9-1-1.

➤ Look at the Medical Emergencies Box.

➤ What medical emergency is the person reporting?

➤ Number from 1 to 6 in your notebook. Write the emergency that matches the situation.

EXAMPLE: *1. choking*

What is this person reporting?

1. My son was eating popcorn. Suddenly he grabbed his throat. He can't speak and he can't breathe.

2. My son found my blood pressure pills. He thought they were candy. He just ate a handful of the pills. I can't wake him up!

3. My neighbour was cutting wood with an electric saw. He just cut his hand. We can't stop the bleeding. He says one of his fingers is missing!

4. My baby was playing with my car keys. She just put the keys into an electrical outlet. Please help me!

5. I left my baby in the bathtub for a few minutes. I just found him with his face in the water. He isn't breathing!

6. My mother-in-law was going downstairs. She just fell! She can't get up and she has a lot of pain in her hip.

Medical Emergencies

choking	a fall	heavy bleeding	drowning
poisoning	a cut	an electric shock	

YOUR TURN

➤ Think of other medical emergencies.

➤ How would you describe the situation to the emergency operator?

An Emergency Admission Form

 READING 2

When a patient is admitted into the hospital emergency, the person at the admitting desk will ask many questions. You need to understand the questions and give accurate answers. Here is a section of an admission form.

➤ Can you read and understand the following admission form?

ARLINGTON GENERAL HOSPITAL
Emergency Admission Form

Patient Name: Cantafio Franco Joe	Time & Date of Admission:
Last Given Names	Hour: 2 p.m.
Phone No. 488-9870	Day: 15 Month: 02 Year: 2005

Patient Address: 1307 Prairie Rose Street	Winnipeg	MB	R4M 2L8
Street	City	Province	Postal Code

Gender: Male	Date of Birth: 19/06/58	Marital Status: Married
	D/M/Y	Medical Plan No. 654 876 123

Other Health Insurance Plan Name & No. Blue Star 5554321

Family Physician: Dr. James Beeson	Phone No. 775-3456		
Nearest Relative: Mario Cantafio	Relationship: Brother	Relative Notified: ☒ Yes ☐ No	Police Contacted: ☐ Yes ☒ No

Patient's Religion: Catholic

Relative's Address: 380 Oak Street Winnipeg, Manitoba	Relative's Phone No. 886-4321

Describe Nature of Accident:
Left hand was caught in wire production machine. Heavy bleeding occurred.

Date, Hour, Place of Accident:
February 15, 2005   1:15 p.m.
Central Metal Works
Winnipeg, Manitoba

Information Taken By: Rhoda Birch

Checking for Understanding

➤ Answer the following questions in your notebook.

1. What time was Franco admitted?
2. Is he married?
3. Who is his nearest relative?
4. What happened to Franco?
5. Was a relative notified?
6. Where did this accident happen?

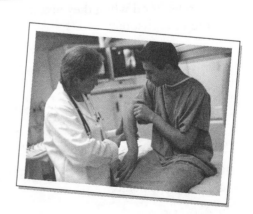

Cont'd

Talking It Over: Asking for Information

➤ Use the key word in each section of the form to help you make a question. Examples of key words are *patient name, phone number, patient address,* etc.

➤ Practise with a partner. Student A is the admitting clerk. Student B gives the patient information.

➤ Practise with Franco's information. Then try again with your own information.

QUESTIONS WITH THE VERB "TO BE"

Question Word	To Be	Rest of Sentence
Who	+ is/are	your/his name?
What	was/were	you/he born?
Where		the accident?
When		your/his nearest relative?
		the cause of the accident?
		your/his family physician

EXAMPLE: Student A: *When were you born?*
                   OR *When was he born?*

            Student B: *June 19, 1958*

            Student A: *What is your phone number?*
                   OR *What is his phone number?*

            Student B: *488-9870*

 page 47 Do WB 6. Asking for Personal Information at Emergency

 Using an Emergency Admission Form

FOCUS ON GRAMMAR

USING IMPERATIVES TO GIVE INSTRUCTIONS

When you phone the emergency operator, you are going to hear instructions. The operator will often use the imperative. An imperative is a sentence that begins with a verb and has no subject. Directions and instructions are more easily understood when they are given in the imperative. We use imperatives for different reasons:

Run cold water over the burn.	→	Giving advice
Loosen his clothing.	→	Giving instructions or directions
Relax. You're doing fine.	→	Encouraging someone
Don't move the person. It's dangerous.	→	Giving a warning
Come to the waiting room and meet the doctor.	→	Issuing an invitation

An imperative sentence uses the following word order:

(Do + not)	Base Verb	Object	Place	Time
	Run	cold water	over the burn	for ten minutes.
Don't	apply	ice.		
Never	apply	ice.		
Never is usually used for advice, a general rule or a warning. *Don't (do not)* is used for instructions for an immediate situation. *Don't and never* come at the beginning of an imperative sentence.				

PART A

Ryan:	Mom! Danny fell down the stairs. His body is all twisted.
Mom:	Stay calm. Don't panic. I'll call 9-1-1.

➤ Read the dialogue between the 9-1-1 operator and Ryan's mom.

➤ Make a list of all the instructions that the operator gives her.

9-1-1 operator:	Keep him still. Don't move him.
Mom:	Don't move him? But he's on the floor.
9-1-1 operator:	Place a blanket lightly over him. It's really important not to move him.
Mom:	What should I do next?
9-1-1 operator:	Place rolled towels around his head.
Mom:	Rolled towels around his head?
9-1-1 operator:	Yes, rolled towels will keep his head still. It is important to keep his head still. Just stay calm. The ambulance is on the way.

PART B

➤ Read the following positive and negative statements.

➤ Match the statements that are related.

EXAMPLE: *1. e*

Positive

1. Cover burned area with a clean cloth or sterile dressing.
2. Cool the skin with cold water.
3. Tell the person to lie still.
4. Stay with the person.
5. Blot the burned area gently.

Negative

a) Don't leave the victim alone.
b) Don't rub the burned skin.
c) Don't apply lotions, ointment or fat to cool the burn.
d) Don't move the person.
e) Don't cover the burn with plastic.

YOUR TURN

> Think about some positive and negative statements to give advice in different emergencies.

> EXAMPLE: If the person is unconscious, cover him. *(positive)*
> If the person is injured, don't move her. *(negative)*

 page 48 Do WB 7. Using Imperatives to Give Instructions

A Pamphlet about Prevention

 READING 3

When we go to emergency for help, the hospital will first treat the emergency problem. Then they will often talk with the patient and family about ways to prevent future emergency situations.

> First, read about an emergency situation.

EMERGENCY SITUATION

Mohammad Shaqi is a seven-year-old boy from Iran. One day at school, he traded his pita for a bag of peanuts. Mmm, they tasted good. But almost immediately his lips began to swell and he was choking for air.

At the hospital his mother learned that her son had a reaction to the peanuts. He has a very serious allergy to peanuts. The hospital gave Mohammad's mother a pamphlet with information about peanut allergies.

> Before you read the pamphlet, think about the information that you know and you want to know about peanut allergies.

 page 49 Do WB 8. Peanut Allergy

A Peanut Allergy

What should I know about a peanut allergy?

One in 50 children and one in 200 adults have an allergy to peanuts.

Children with a peanut allergy can develop allergies to other nuts.

Children do not usually outgrow a peanut allergy.

What is it?

It's an allergy to peanuts that can be life threatening.

What are the symptoms of a peanut allergy?

The symptoms happen just after eating or having contact with a peanut product.

The symptoms are:

- itchy or swollen lips, mouth, eyes or tongue
- tightness in mouth, chest or throat
- difficulty breathing or swallowing
- choking, coughing
- runny nose or voice change
- vomiting, nausea, diarrhea, stomach pains
- dizziness, chills
- loss of consciousness, coma, death

What can I do if I think my child is allergic to peanuts?

- Teach your child how to ask about peanut products when he is eating away from home.
- Never buy foods without checking the label for peanut products.
- Ask questions about food preparation methods when eating away from home.
- Make sure other people know about your child's allergy, including the school.

When do I call a doctor?

If you think you or your child is having an allergic reaction to peanuts, call a doctor or ambulance immediately.

Feel Empowered

When you want to check about peanut products in food, ask, "Does this food have any trace of peanut products in it?"

 Using Questions to Get Information

Filling in an Accident Report Form at Work

If there is a medical emergency at work, we sometimes have to fill in a form to report the accident.

➤ Read the information, so that you know how to fill in this kind of a form.

ACCIDENT REPORT FORM AT WORK

This form is kept by the employer as a permanent record.

Fill this form in at work.

Name of Injured Person ___Tom Chan___

Date and Time of Injury ___July 25, 2005 at 3:00 p.m.___

Cause of the Injury ___Tripped and fell while carrying heavy equipment___

What was the nature of the injury? ___Broken ankle___

Name(s) of Witnesses to the Injury ___Maria Santos___

Signature of Supervisor ___Marco J. Hoffman___

Signature of Injured Worker ___Tom Chan___

Injured worker should keep one copy and give the employer a second copy.

Checking for Understanding

➤ Are these statements *true* or *false*? Write *T* or *F* in your notebook.

1. Tom should fill in this form at the hospital.
2. He should fill in two copies.
3. The employer should keep a copy.
4. Someone saw what happened to Tom.
5. Tom cut his ankle.

Culture Note

Whenever you have any kind of accident at work, fill in an accident report form to protect yourself and keep one copy.

 page 50 Do WB 9. Filling in an Accident Report Form

Talking to a 9-1-1 Operator

BREAKING IT DOWN

In an emergency situation, there is an order to the dialogue and the functions of the sentences.

Action	→ Language Function
We ask for help.	Requesting assistance
We say what is happening.	Describing a situation
We say that we will help.	Offering assistance
We tell someone that it is dangerous.	Advising someone of danger
We tell someone how to do something.	Giving instructions

➤ Read the dialogue between a 9-1-1 operator and a caller. Think about the language they use.

➤ Look at the list of language functions.

➤ Choose the function to describe the language that each speaker uses.

EXAMPLE: *1. b*

9-1-1 operator:	**What is the emergency?**
1. Caller:	My husband just fell off a ladder and he can't move.
2. 9-1-1 Operator:	Keep him still. Don't move your husband before the ambulance arrives.
3. Caller:	What should I do? Can you help me?
4. 9-1-1 Operator:	Be careful. Moving him could injure his back even more.
5. Caller:	He is conscious and lying on the ground.
6. 9-1-1 Operator:	The attendants will help you when the ambulance arrives.

Language Functions

a) Requesting assistance

b) Describing a situation

c) Offering assistance

d) Advising someone of danger

e) Giving instructions

page 51 Do WB 10. Word Bank

Did You Know ...?

Situations in a Medical Emergency

➤ Work with a partner. What would you say in each situation?

➤ Share your answers with the whole group.

➤ Use this language practice to help you develop a dialogue between you and a 9-1-1 operator.

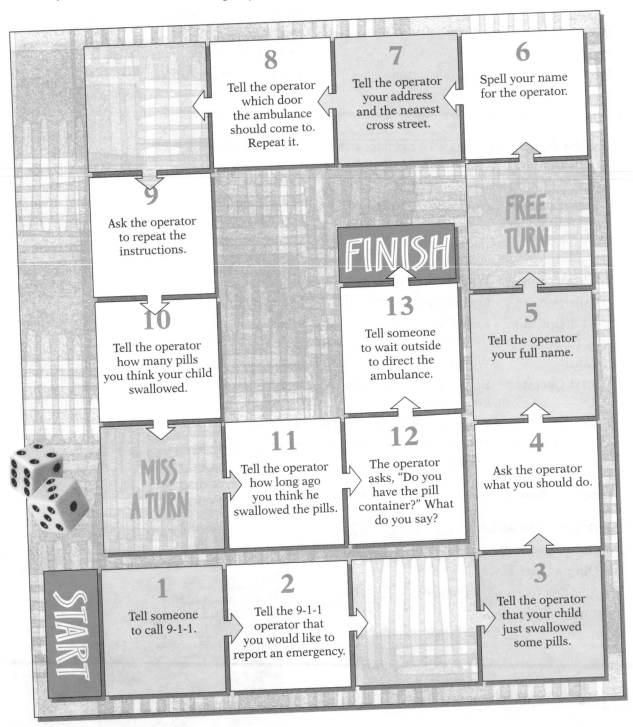

8
Tell the operator which door the ambulance should come to. Repeat it.

7
Tell the operator your address and the nearest cross street.

6
Spell your name for the operator.

9
Ask the operator to repeat the instructions.

FREE TURN

FINISH

13
Tell someone to wait outside to direct the ambulance.

5
Tell the operator your full name.

10
Tell the operator how many pills you think your child swallowed.

MISS A TURN

11
Tell the operator how long ago you think he swallowed the pills.

12
The operator asks, "Do you have the pill container?" What do you say?

4
Ask the operator what you should do.

START

1
Tell someone to call 9-1-1.

2
Tell the 9-1-1 operator that you would like to report an emergency.

3
Tell the operator that your child just swallowed some pills.

 page 52 Do WB 11. Learning Progress Check

Dealing with Consumer Problems

Learning Opportunities

As a consumer, you should be as well-informed as possible. You should be able to communicate what you want. You will learn:

- To describe a situation or problem.
- To tell someone what you need.
- To ask someone for assistance.
- To ask someone for an explanation.
- To respond appropriately to direct salespeople.
- To understand when someone offers assistance.
- To read details in a warranty.
- To find information in a warranty registration card.
- To fill out a warranty card.
- To write a letter of complaint.

1 – Won Suk 2 – customer service rep.

"I need a new TV. The picture is distorted."

SETTING THE SCENE

When you buy items or pay for services, you are a consumer. As a consumer, you need language to understand what the seller tells you. You need to be able to ask questions. Consumers read receipts, warranties and signs about store policies. As a consumer, you may want to write a letter if you have problems.

Culture Note

Stores have different return policies. Check carefully before you buy something. Ask, "What is your return policy?"

TALKING IT OVER

1. Describe what you see in the picture.

2. Why do you think the customer is returning the TV?

3. What do you think the sales representative will do about the problem?

HOW ABOUT YOU?

1. Have you ever taken something back to a store?

2. Why did you take it back?

3. How did the store help you?

4. What do people in your community do when they buy something and they want to return it?

WORDS TO THINK ABOUT

1. customer service rep.

2. returns

3. original receipt

4. time limit

5. an exchange

6. return policy

7. the same model

8. defective

9. distorted

Returning a TV to the Store

LISTENING

Listening for Key Information

➤ Listen carefully to the conversation between Won Suk and a customer service representative at the store.

➤ Your teacher will play the dialogue in parts.

➤ Can you hear the *chunks of language* listed below?

➤ While listening, touch each chunk of language as you hear it. Notice how you can hear the new and important information by listening for the stress. The **stressed words** will be **longer, louder and slower** than the other words.

snowy picture

wavy lines

distorted picture

1. the picture is distorted

2. all the time

3. disappointed

4. adjusting the picture

5. pressed some buttons

6. improve the picture quality

7. What does that mean?

8. still bad

9. don't look right

10. original receipt

11. purchased

12. 30-day return policy

13. exchange this one

14. the same model

15. Sight and Sound Electronics

 page 53 Do WB 1. Listening for Key Information

Cont'd

Listening for Details

- ➤ Read the following questions.
- ➤ Listen to the conversation. Write down one or two words to answer each question.
- ➤ Discuss your answers with a partner.

1. Why is Won Suk returning the TV?
2. Who is disappointed?
3. What did her son do to try to improve the picture?
4. Did she remember to bring her original receipt?
5. How long do customers have to return or exchange purchases?
6. Did she exchange her TV or get a refund?

Listening Strategy ♟

Sometimes writing down one or two important words as you listen can help you to remember details.

YOUR TURN

- ➤ Work with a partner.
- ➤ Practise asking each other questions about Won Suk and her consumer problem. Use *chunks of language* for the answers.

Listening for the Gist

Giving Reasons for Returns

When you return an item to the store, you have to explain why you want to return it. The store wants to know the reason. Sometimes, we return an item because it is not suitable. Sometimes, the item is defective.

Your satisfaction is **important** to us.

The TV is too small.	→	The item is not suitable.
The screen goes black.	→	The item is defective.

- ➤ Listen to the customers. They are giving reasons for returning items.
- ➤ Decide why each customer is returning the item. Is it because it is unsuitable or is it because it is defective?
- ➤ Explain your choice.

📖 **page 54** Do WB 2. Giving Reasons for Returns

💻 Talking with a Salesperson

CUSTOMER SERVICE DEPARTMENT

Return Policy Signs

READING 1

Some stores have signs that explain their return policies. Watch for these signs. Check the return policy before you buy.

➤ Look at each of the store signs.

➤ Read the store's return policy.

➤ Now read the story about each customer.

➤ Where do you think each customer shopped?

STORE 1
Sometimes, stores have time limits for returns.

STORE 2
Some stores will not give refunds. They will only give you another item.

STORE 3
Sometimes, you can't get a refund or an exchange.

STORE 4
Some stores will always give you your money back!

Which store did these customers shop at?

1. Dolores always shops at the same store. She has no problems getting her money back. She can always get a refund.

2. Sylvia wanted to return a DVD. She took it back after ten days. They would not give her another DVD. They told her it was not within the store's time limit.

3. Carlos took back a toaster. He asked for his money back. The store offered him a new toaster, but would not return his money.

4. Adam bought a coffee maker on sale. It was 50 percent off. A few days later, he changed his mind. He wanted to exchange it for a bigger one. The store refused to exchange the coffee maker, because it was a sale item.

 page 54 Do WB 3. Asking about a Store Return Policy

Describing a Problem with an Appliance

SPEAKING

To return an appliance, go to Customer Service or the repair counter. Take your sales receipt along and return the appliance in the original box. To help you describe the problem, write down the details on a piece of paper.

➤ Read the conversation below.

➤ Practise the conversation as a whole class and then in pairs.

➤ Look at the words and expressions that are underlined and in bold. Use the information in the suggestion boxes to change the dialogue. Substitute the information for the correct number in the conversation.

Salesperson: May I help you?

Customer: Yes. I bought this **blender**[1] here
about a month ago.[2] Here's my receipt.

Salesperson: What seems to be the problem?

Customer: Well, when I **push the button for low speed,**[3]
the blades won't turn.[4]

Salesperson: If you would like, we can **exchange it for another one.**[5]

Suggestion Boxes

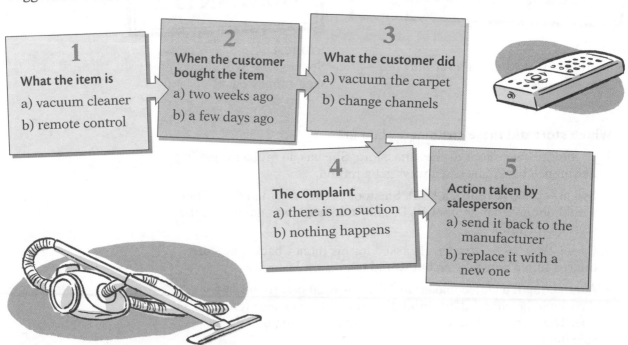

1

What the item is

a) vacuum cleaner

b) remote control

2

When the customer bought the item

a) two weeks ago

b) a few days ago

3

What the customer did

a) vacuum the carpet

b) change channels

4

The complaint

a) there is no suction

b) nothing happens

5

Action taken by salesperson

a) send it back to the manufacturer

b) replace it with a new one

📖 **page 55** Do WB 4. Describing a Problem with an Appliance

Sellers and Consumers

WORD PLAY

There are many words and expressions used by sellers and consumers.

➤ Read the following scenarios and look at the words in **bold**.

➤ Then look at the numbered words in the boxes to the right.

➤ Find a word from the scenario, which has the same meaning.

➤ Make a list of the words in your notebook and write your choices beside each.

EXAMPLE: *A. 1. extra – additional*

Scenario A

Sharon went to Weller's Home Furniture Sale last Saturday. Everything in the store was at least 30 percent **off**. Sharon was looking at an oak coffee table. It had a small scratch on one side. The salesperson told her that it was a floor model. He took an **additional** 10 percent off because the table had a scratch. Sharon **bought** it "**as is**" and she got a receipt that said "Final Sale."

Scenario B

The store wants its customers to be happy with their **merchandise** and service. If something doesn't work, they want you to return the item for an exchange or **a refund.** The store's **policy** is displayed on a large sign. It reads: "**Satisfaction Guaranteed.**"

Scenario C

Bill and Judy purchased a new sofa and chair at Stewart's Furniture Store. The price tag read: $1299 for **the set.** When they saw the total bill it was $212 more. They **inquired** about the difference in the price. The salesperson reminded them of the taxes and a $30 delivery **charge**. Next time, they will remember to **figure out** the extra charges ahead of time.

Words

1. extra
2. purchased
3. reduced
4. with the defect

5. We want our customers to be happy.
6. products
7. money that is given back
8. rule

9. asked questions
10. the matching pieces
11. calculate
12. fee

 page 57 Do WB 5. Describing Consumer Problems

UNDERSTANDING ENGLISH SYLLABLES AND RHYTHM

A syllable is a small part of a word that has one beat or one tap. Every syllable has one vowel sound.

PART A

➤ Listen and repeat each word.

➤ Tap each syllable with your finger or pen.

➤ When you hear the word, listen for the syllable that is stressed. The stressed syllable will be **longer** and **louder** than the unstressed syllables.

1 syllable	2 syllables	3 syllables	4 syllables
it	broken	defective	situation
in	promised	merchandise	additional
scratch	reduced	furniture	appropriate
bought	receipt	operate	satisfaction

PART B

➤ Listen and repeat the following words.

➤ Now cover the words. Listen again. Repeat each word and tap the syllables in rhythm.

➤ Copy the words into your notebook. Write the number of syllables.

EXAMPLE: *vacuum – 2 syllables*

1. manufacturer
2. receipt
3. blade
4. automatically
5. steam
6. promised
7. price
8. satisfaction
9. guaranteed

 Understanding Syllables and Rhythm

ASKING AND ANSWERING YES/NO QUESTIONS

There are two kinds of *yes/no* questions: an *action verb* question and a *be verb* question. You answer an *action verb* question differently than a *be verb* question.

Question Pattern		Question	Short Answer
An *action verb* question is made up of:			
Do/does		Do you have any problems with your TV?	Yes, I **do.** / No, I **don't.**
	+ subject + main verb + all other words?	Does Won Suk have a problem?	Yes, she **does.** / No, she **doesn't.**
Did		Did Won Suk go back to the store?	Yes, she **did.** / No, she **didn't.**
Will		Will they exchange her TV for a new one?	Yes, they **will.** / No, they **won't.**
Can		Can she get a new TV right away?	Yes, she **can.** / No, she **can't.**
A *be verb* question is made up of:			
Am/is/are	+ subject + all other words?	Are you a consumer?	Yes, I **am.** / No, I**'m** not
		Is it defective?	Yes, it **is.** / No, it **isn't.**
Was/were		Were you at the store yesterday?	Yes, I **was.** / No, I **wasn't.**

➤ Work with a partner to answer the following questions.

➤ Choose a yes/no answer from the Answer Box.

1. Is Won Suk's TV defective?

2. Did she buy her TV a few weeks ago?

3. Does she have a warranty?

4. Can she return her TV?

5. Will the store exchange her TV?

6. Do you need to have a receipt for a return?

7. Are insurance and transportation covered under the guarantee?

8. Does the warranty apply if she tries to fix the TV herself?

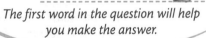

Learning Strategy
The first word in the question will help you make the answer.

Answer Box

a) No, they aren't.	e) No, it doesn't.
b) Yes, she does.	f) Yes, it will.
c) Yes, you do.	g) Yes, it is.
d) Yes, she did.	h) Yes, she can.

📖 **page 58** Do WB 6. Answering Yes/No Questions

USING CONDITIONAL SENTENCES

Use a conditional (an *if-clause*) to talk about something that is possible
in the present or future.

If-Clause (Simple Present)	Result Clause (Will + Base Verb)
If I fix the TV myself,	the warranty will not apply.
If I have a full warranty,	the store will replace or refund my money.

It is possible to write the result clause before the if-clause. You don't need
a comma.

Result Clause	If Clause
The warranty will not apply	if I fix the TV myself.
The store will replace or refund my money	if I have a full warranty.

➤ Work with a partner.

➤ Read the information about kinds of warranties
to understand the differences.

➤ Complete each **if-clause** with a result.

➤ Write each complete conditional sentence in
your notebook.

➤ Then write these sentences in your notebook
with the result clause before the if-clause.
Remember, you don't need a comma.

Learning Strategy

*Reading the words in bold or italics helps
you find important information.*

Won Suk learned that there are two kinds
of warranties: a "full warranty" and a
"limited warranty."

A **full warranty** means that the company will

• provide free warranty service to anyone
owning the item during the warranty
time period.

• provide a replacement or money refund
if the item cannot be repaired.

• provide warranty service without the
customer returning a warranty registration
card.

A **limited warranty** means that the customer
will be responsible for some of the repair costs.

For an item sold "**as is**" there will be **no
warranty.**

If-clause

1. If the store can't repair my TV,

2. If you forget to send in the warranty card,

3. If there is a limited warranty,

4. If my TV develops a problem within
the warranty time period,

5. If I buy a TV marked "as is,"

6. If I have a full warranty,

A Warranty

READING 2

Won Suk's TV isn't working. She bought it two weeks ago. It is still under warranty. Won Suk has the receipt. She's going to take the TV back to the store.

➤ Read the warranty carefully. Then do the activity in your workbook.

This is the warranty for Won Suk's TV.

Mashiba of Canada Ltd.
Limited 90-Day Warranty

The company guarantees this TV for 90 days from date of purchase. — Time limit is 90 days from date of buying it.

If the TV doesn't work, return it to the store — Condition
where you bought it. The store will replace parts — What will happen?
or exchange it for the same model. No charge — What is covered?
for parts and labour.

This guarantee does not cover insurance and — What is not paid for?
transportation costs to service station.

The guarantee will be void if you try to fix — Condition
the TV.

Mashiba offers a 1-year limited warranty on parts. Buyer must — Fine Print:
pay all labour charges after 90 days. It is necessary to read the very small print. It contains some very important information.

📖 **page 59** Do WB 7. Understanding a Warranty

Filling in a Warranty Registration Card

READING 3

WRITING

Many consumer products come with a warranty card from the manufacturer. This is a written promise that the product is good quality and will work properly. The warranty registration card should be filled out soon after you purchase the item. Filling out the warranty registration card can help you get more efficient service in case there are any problems with the product.

➤ Read Won Suk's warranty registration card.

➤ Answer the questions that follow. Then practise filling in a registration card in your workbook.

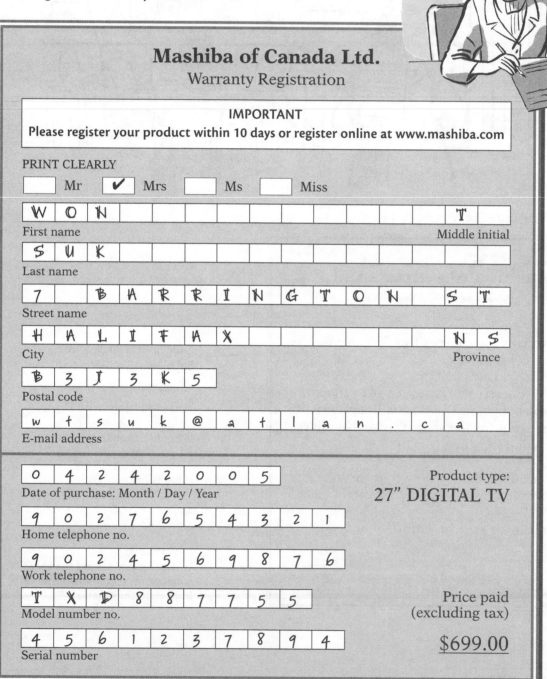

Mashiba of Canada Ltd.
Warranty Registration

IMPORTANT
Please register your product within 10 days or register online at www.mashiba.com

PRINT CLEARLY

☐ Mr   ✔ Mrs   ☐ Ms   ☐ Miss

| W | O | N | | | | | | | | | | T | |
First name   Middle initial

| S | U | K | | | | | | | | | | | |
Last name

| 7 | | B | A | R | R | I | N | G | T | O | N | | S | T |
Street name

| H | A | L | I | F | A | X | | | | | | | N | S |
City   Province

| B | 3 | J | 3 | K | 5 |
Postal code

| w | t | s | u | k | @ | a | t | l | a | n | . | c | a |
E-mail address

| 0 | 4 | 2 | 4 | 2 | 0 | 0 | 5 |
Date of purchase: Month / Day / Year

| 9 | 0 | 2 | 7 | 6 | 5 | 4 | 3 | 2 | 1 |
Home telephone no.

| 9 | 0 | 2 | 4 | 5 | 6 | 9 | 8 | 7 | 6 |
Work telephone no.

| T | X | D | 8 | 8 | 7 | 7 | 5 | 5 |
Model number no.

| 4 | 5 | 6 | 1 | 2 | 3 | 7 | 8 | 9 | 4 |
Serial number

Product type:
27" DIGITAL TV

Price paid
(excluding tax)

$699.00

Checking for Understanding

➤ Work with a partner and answer these questions orally.

1. What city is Won Suk from?
2. Is Won Suk married?
3. When did Won Suk buy this product?
4. How can she register with Mashiba?
5. Can she fill out the warranty card online?
6. What is Won Suk's phone number at work?
7. Do you need to print on the form?
8. What are the first three digits of the serial number?
9. Does she live in New Brunswick?
10. Did Won Suk pay exactly $699 for her TV?

YOUR TURN

➤ Write down two more questions that you could ask about Won Suk's warranty registration.

 page 61 Do WB 8. Filling in a Warranty Registration Card

Dealing with Direct Sales Representatives

SPEAKING

Sales representatives often phone or visit our homes to sell us products. We need language to refuse or ask for time to think about it.

➤ Practise the model dialogue with a partner to help you learn what to say.

➤ Then try each situation. Take turns being the direct seller and the customer.

➤ Present one of the dialogues to the class.

Model Dialogue

Direct Seller: Good afternoon. I'm with Feel Safe Home Alarms. We've got a special price on our alarms right now.

Customer: Really? I'm not sure we need an alarm system.

Direct Seller: Well, it's a very good price—three months free of charge. All you need to do is sign this contract.

Customer: What happens if I want to change my mind?

Direct Seller: You have 24 hours to think it over after you sign the contract.

Customer: Is your company listed with the Better Business Bureau?

Direct Seller: Yes, we are. If you want to check, you can call them.

Cont'd

Situation 1

Direct Seller:	Introduce yourself as George Neilson and tell the customer that you are representing the Canadian Cancer Prevention Society.
Customer:	Say "oh" or "ok" as you wait for them to give you more information.
Direct Seller:	Say you are selling healthy cookies to raise money.
Customer:	Ask for some identification.
Direct Seller:	Say that you have identification and show your badge.
Customer:	Ask him to leave an envelope. Tell him you want to think about it.
Direct Seller:	Say there's no problem. Say, "There you are" as you hand the homeowner an envelope.

Situation 2

Direct Seller:	Introduce yourself as Don. Say that you are with Johnson Carpet Cleaning. Say that you can do all of their carpets for $98.99.
Customer:	Tell him that you are eating dinner at the moment.
Direct Seller:	Say that you'll only take a minute of their time. Ask how many rooms they have.
Customer:	Tell him firmly that you're not interested.
Direct Seller:	Wish the homeowner a good evening.

Culture Note

You usually have 24 hours to cancel a direct sale.

Situation 3

Direct Seller:	Tell the homeowner that you are sorry to bother them but you see that their windows are pretty old.
Customer:	Agree and say that you know your house is getting older.
Direct Seller:	Say that you have a crew working in the area. Tell the owner that you can start to replace the windows right away.
Customer:	Ask for an estimate. Tell him that you want to talk it over with your husband (wife). Ask for the names of a couple of references.
Direct Seller:	Say, "Yes." Tell the homeowner that your company replaced windows next door. Suggest talking to them.
Customer:	Tell him that you prefer to take your time before you spend a lot of money.
Direct Seller:	Say that you are getting very busy. Tell the homeowner that they will have to decide pretty soon.

A Letter of Complaint

READING 4

WRITING

If a consumer has not received the service expected, a letter of complaint may help get results. The letter must include details about the product and a clear statement of the problem.

➤ Read Julie's letter of complaint.

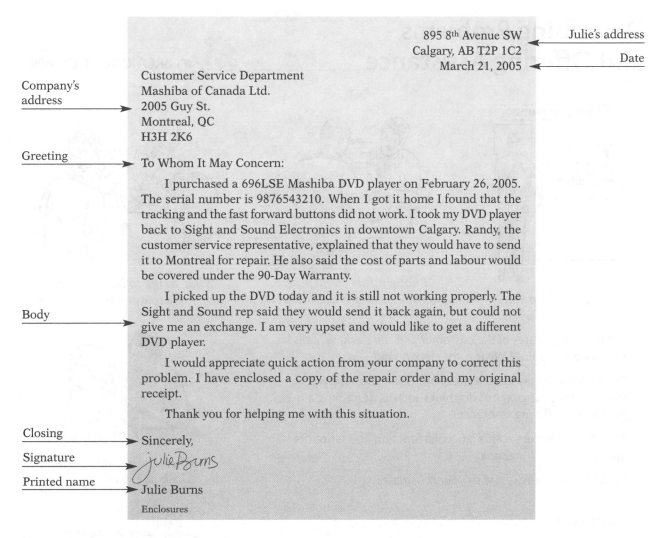

Julie's address →

Date →

895 8th Avenue SW
Calgary, AB T2P 1C2
March 21, 2005

Company's address →

Customer Service Department
Mashiba of Canada Ltd.
2005 Guy St.
Montreal, QC
H3H 2K6

Greeting →

To Whom It May Concern:

Body →

I purchased a 696LSE Mashiba DVD player on February 26, 2005. The serial number is 9876543210. When I got it home I found that the tracking and the fast forward buttons did not work. I took my DVD player back to Sight and Sound Electronics in downtown Calgary. Randy, the customer service representative, explained that they would have to send it to Montreal for repair. He also said the cost of parts and labour would be covered under the 90-Day Warranty.

I picked up the DVD today and it is still not working properly. The Sight and Sound rep said they would send it back again, but could not give me an exchange. I am very upset and would like to get a different DVD player.

I would appreciate quick action from your company to correct this problem. I have enclosed a copy of the repair order and my original receipt.

Thank you for helping me with this situation.

Closing →

Sincerely,

Signature →

Julie Burns

Printed name →

Julie Burns

Enclosures

Checking for Understanding

➤ Discuss these questions with a partner.

1. Who wrote this letter?
2. When did she purchase her DVD player?
3. What is the model number of the DVD player?
4. What is the problem with Julie's DVD player?
5. Where did Sight and Sound send her DVD?
6. Did she have to pay for parts and labour?
7. Why is she writing to Mashiba?
8. Which line states that she wants fast service?

YOUR TURN

➤ Follow the model letter to write a letter of complaint using your own information.

➤ Remember to state the problem clearly. Also, include the product brand name, model, serial number, date and place of purchase.

 page 62 Do WB 9. Tips for Smart Consumers

 Letter of Complaint to a Store ¦ Letter of Complaint to a Rental Agency ¦

Describing Problems
and Offering Assistance

BREAKING IT DOWN

"How can I help you?"

*"I bought this blender here a
month ago and it doesn't work."*

*"What seems to be the problem?
Can you explain what is wrong?"*

➤ Look at the pictures of the customer and the clerk. What is
the customer doing? What is the clerk doing?

➤ Read what they say in each situation. Think about how
they are using language to do things such as describing a
problem or offering assistance.

➤ Match each picture with a language function and write the
answers in your notebook.

➤ Compare your answers with your classmates.

EXAMPLE: *1. c*

*"When I push the button,
the blade won't turn."*

Language Functions

a) Describing a problem

b) Asking for an explanation

c) Offering assistance

d) Saying what you need

"I need a new blender."

YOUR TURN

➤ Think of an appliance or electronic equipment problem that
you might have.

➤ How would you describe the problem to a clerk?
EXAMPLE: *This TV has no sound.*

➤ How would you say what you need or want?
EXAMPLE: *I would like to get a refund.*

➤ Write a dialogue between you and a clerk.

"I will get one down for you."

Returning Items at a Store

➤ Work with a partner. Choose a picture of an appliance or electronic equipment from a flyer.

➤ Think of a reason that you might return the item.

➤ Write a dialogue about returning an item or finding out about a warranty.

➤ Use the examples below for ideas.

➤ Practise the dialogue and then present it to the class.

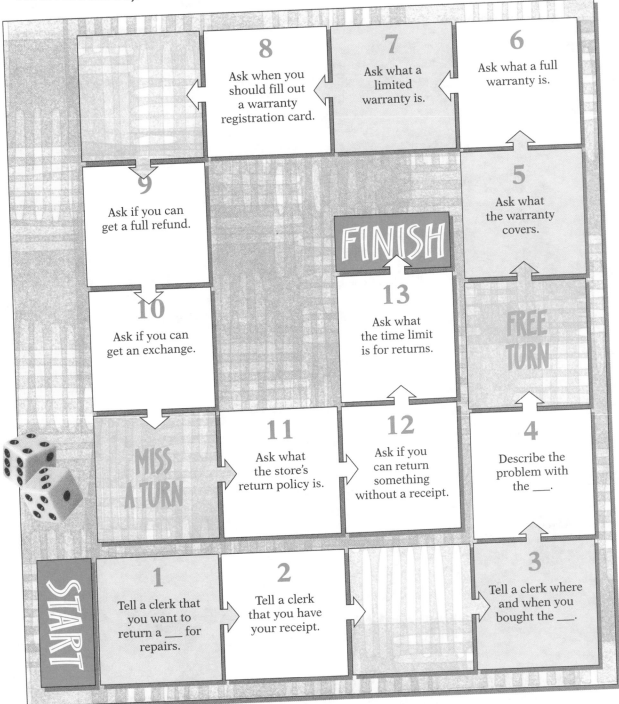

8 Ask when you should fill out a warranty registration card.

7 Ask what a limited warranty is.

6 Ask what a full warranty is.

9 Ask if you can get a full refund.

5 Ask what the warranty covers.

FINISH

10 Ask if you can get an exchange.

13 Ask what the time limit is for returns.

FREE TURN

MISS A TURN

11 Ask what the store's return policy is.

12 Ask if you can return something without a receipt.

4 Describe the problem with the ___.

START

1 Tell a clerk that you want to return a ___ for repairs.

2 Tell a clerk that you have your receipt.

3 Tell a clerk where and when you bought the ___.

📖 **page 63** Do WB 10. Word Bank   **page 64** Do WB 11. Learning Progress Check

Getting Ready to Look for Work

Learning Opportunities

Can you describe your job duties? Do you know how to talk about your job training and experience? In this unit, you will have the opportunity to practise some of the language skills you need to get ready to look for work. You will learn:

- To describe skills and abilities.
- To describe employment goals.
- To talk about occupations and work experience.
- To give work preferences.
- To describe job duties.
- To listen for specific information.
- To locate information about jobs in a classified ad.
- To fill in an application for employment counselling.

"I want to work as a vet again."

SETTING THE SCENE

When you are getting ready to find a job, it is important to take some time to think about the kind of work you like to do. You should also think about your skills and experience. Decide what your short-term goals are. Decide what your long-term goals are. Remember there are often services in the community that can help you get ready to look for work.

Culture Note

Many people volunteer in the community to gain Canadian work experience.

TALKING IT OVER

1. What do you see in the picture?
2. What do you think the teacher and the student are discussing?
3. What questions do you think the teacher asked?
4. What answers do you think the student gave?

HOW ABOUT YOU?

1. What is your occupation?
2. What skills do you have?
3. What work experience do you have?
4. What are your plans or goals?

WORDS TO THINK ABOUT

1. job skills
2. abilities
3. occupation
4. experience
5. short-term goals
6. long-term goals
7. veterinarian
8. to set goals
9. to volunteer

Getting Ready to Look for Work

 LISTENING

Listening for Key Information

➤ Listen carefully to the conversation between Wesson and his teacher.

➤ Your teacher will play the dialogue in parts.

➤ Can you hear the *chunks of language* listed below?

➤ While listening, touch each chunk of language as you hear it. Notice how you can hear the new and important information by listening for the stress. The **stressed words** will be **longer, louder and slower** than the other words.

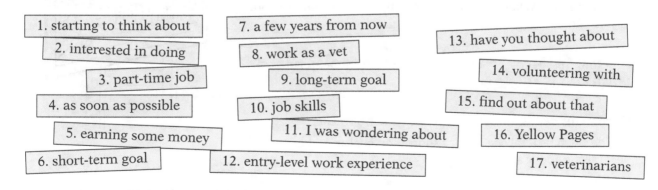

1. starting to think about
2. interested in doing
3. part-time job
4. as soon as possible
5. earning some money
6. short-term goal
7. a few years from now
8. work as a vet
9. long-term goal
10. job skills
11. I was wondering about
12. entry-level work experience
13. have you thought about
14. volunteering with
15. find out about that
16. Yellow Pages
17. veterinarians

 page 65 Do WB 1. Listening for Key Information

Cont'd

Listening for Details

➤ Read the following questions. Ask yourself what specific information you are listening for.

➤ Listen for the details in the conversation. Write down one or two words in your notebook to answer each question.

➤ Discuss your answers with a partner.

1. What is Wesson starting to think about?
2. When does he want to start working?
3. Why does he need a part-time job?
4. What is Wesson's long-term goal?
5. What did Wesson work with before coming to Canada?
6. What does his teacher suggest?
7. Where can Wesson get a list of veterinarians?

Veterinarians **360**

Bloor Mobile Veterinary Services
65 Collingwood Blvd.......555-6410

East York Animal Clinic
615 O'Connell Drive.......555-5462

Gerrard Animal Hospital
1300 Queen St.......555-2610

Lennox Veterinary Practice
65 Lennox Ave.......555-8999

YOUR TURN

➤ Work with a partner.

➤ Practise asking each other questions about Wesson.

➤ Answer the questions with a couple of words or a phrase.

Listening for the Gist

Short-Term or Long-Term Goals

When you are getting ready to look for work, it is important to think about your goals. What are your short-term goals? What are your long-term goals?

I want to find a job right away.	→	Short-term goal
I want to work as a vet in the future.	→	Long-term goal

➤ Listen to the discussion between Wesson and his teacher.

➤ Decide when he is talking about a short-term goal and when he is talking about a long-term goal.

➤ Explain your choice.

Learning Strategy

Setting goals is a good strategy in language learning and in finding a job.

📖 **page 66** Do WB 2. Talking about Goals and Past Experience

Thinking about Our Values

As Wesson talked about what kind of work he wanted to do, his teacher asked him about his values. These are the ideas or beliefs that are important to us.

➤ Read about Wesson's values. Which values will make him a good veterinarian? Do you think any of his values will be a problem in his job?

➤ Discuss with your classmates.

Wesson's Values

- I believe that doing a job well is very important.
- I believe that you should treat animals with respect.
- It's important to have a supervisor that I can work well with.
- It's important to continue to develop new skills.
- It's important to have a permanent position.
- It's very important to be at home with my family in the evenings and on weekends.
- It's important to work as a licensed veterinarian.

YOUR TURN

➤ Say which values are important to you.

➤ Discuss why they are important. Use **because** in your answers.

EXAMPLE: It is important to earn a good salary **because** *I have a big family.*

1. It is important to earn a good salary *because* ...
2. It's important to do excellent work *because* ...
3. It's important to have a regular routine *because* ...
4. It's important to help other people *because* ...
5. It's important to help protect our environment *because* ...
6. It's important to be able to work well with my co-workers *because* ...

➤ Add your own ideas.

7. It's important to ... *because* ...
8. It's important to ... *because* ...

Describing Strengths

READING 2

➤ Read the section of a reference letter about Wesson. A reference letter is a letter about you as a worker.

➤ What are Wesson's strengths? How does the employer describe them?

➤ Make a list of words that the employer uses to describe Wesson's strengths.

➤ Discuss with a partner.

We had the pleasure to work with Wesson and found he works well with livestock. He is very hard-working and usually identifies problems quickly. He treats clients and their animals in a comforting manner. We can rely on Wesson to do the job. In an emergency situation, he stays calm and knows what to do. He gives clear directions if he needs assistance. Overall, Wesson is an excellent veterinarian.

Santiago Dairy Farms

 page 66 Do WB 3. Describing Strengths

Feel Empowered

If you want a reference letter from your employer, ask: "Would you be willing to write me a reference letter?"

YOUR TURN

➤ Think about your work experience.

➤ What are some ways that an employer has described your strengths?

PRONUNCIATION POINTER

WORD STRESS AND THE –TION ENDING

PART A

➤ Listen to each pair of words. Find the stressed syllable.

➤ Look at the list of verbs. In which syllable do you find the stress? Is there a pattern?

➤ Now look at the list of nouns with a *–tion* ending. Where is the stressed syllable in relation to the *–tion* sound?

Verbs	Nouns
1. com**mun**icate	communi**ca**tion
2. pre**pare**	prepar**a**tion
3. in**form**	infor**ma**tion
4. examine	examination
5. explain	explanation
6. associate	association
7. invite	invitation
8. install	installation
9. apply	application
10. participate	participation

PART B

➤ Work with a partner and make questions with the word lists (verbs and nouns).

➤ Ask each other questions and make up answers.

➤ Share these sentences with the class.

➤ Remember to stress the correct syllables as you read your sentences.

➤ Listen to your classmates. Are they using these words in a way that is new to you?

EXAMPLES:

Student A

*What do you **examine** carefully before you buy?*

*What did you **apply** for?*

*Are you writing an **invitation**?*

Student B

I examine fruit carefully before I buy it.

I applied for English language training.

Yes. I'm writing an invitation for my daughter's birthday party.

 Word Stress and –TION

FOCUS ON GRAMMAR

USING "PREFER" TO TALK ABOUT PREFERENCES

You can use the gerund or the infinitive to talk about what kind of job you prefer to do.

	Question: Do you prefer ...?	Answer
Prefer + gerund	Do you prefer **working** with people or animals?	I prefer **working** ...
Prefer + infinitive	Do you prefer **to work** alone or with people?	I prefer **to work** ...

PART A

➤ Work with a partner.

➤ Read the following questions out loud.

➤ Say your answer first with the gerund and then with the infinitive.

➤ Take turns asking and answering the questions.

EXAMPLES:

Student A

*Do you **prefer to work** alone or with many people?*

*Do you **prefer working** alone or with many people?*

Student B

*I **prefer to work** alone.*

*I **prefer working** alone.*

1. Do you prefer to help people or to work with machines?

2. Do you prefer to try new things or to do the same thing most of the time?

3. Do you prefer to help people or to fix mechanical problems?

4. Do you prefer to work at a desk most of the day or to move around most of the day?

5. Do you prefer to plan your own work or to receive organized work?

6. Do you prefer to work regular hours or to work shift work?

7. Do you prefer to work under pressure or to work with little or no pressure?

8. Do you prefer to work on one thing at a time or to work on several things at the same time?

9. Do you prefer to take chances and risks or to take few risks?

PART B

➤ Ask the questions again using the gerund.

EXAMPLE: *Do you prefer **helping** people or **working** with machines?*

Sometimes people don't answer in full sentences. This language is less formal.

➤ Ask the questions another time. This time, answer them using short answers.

EXAMPLES:

Student A

*Do you **prefer to work** alone or with many people?*

*Do you **prefer working** alone or with many people?*

Student B

To work alone.

Working alone.

📖 **page 67** Do WB 4. Using "Prefer" to Talk about Preferences

Describing Job Responsibilities

WORD PLAY

➤ Look at the job titles and illustrations.

➤ Match the job titles with the responsibilities of the job.

EXAMPLE: *1. g*

Job Titles

1. veterinarian
2. nurse
3. plumber
4. carpenter
5. mechanic
6. chef
7. child-care worker
8. entrepreneur
9. counsellor
10. assembler
11. electrician
12. journalist
13. waiter
14. hairdresser
15. accountant
16. farmer

Responsibilities

a) fixes engines
b) listens carefully and offers advice
c) installs wiring
d) is in charge of young children
e) reports the news
f) starts a new business
g) treats sick or injured animals
h) fixes pipes
i) puts things together
j) serves food to customers
k) builds houses or furniture
l) checks vital signs
m) plans and prepares meals
n) gives perms
o) keeps records
p) plows the fields

YOUR TURN

➤ Work with a partner to practise a short dialogue about each job.

EXAMPLE: Student A: *What is your occupation?*
Student B: *I am a carpenter.*
Student A: *What do you do?*
Student B: *I build houses.*

➤ Think of one more duty for each worker and write it in your notebook.

 Describing Job Duties

Talking with a Job Counsellor

SPEAKING

As you get ready to look for work, you may meet with a job counsellor.
The counsellor may ask you to talk about what you did in your previous job.

➤ Work with a partner.

➤ Practise the sample dialogue.

➤ Now, add one more responsibility for each job.

EXAMPLE: Nurse: • check vital signs
                    • take blood pressure
                    • give medication
                    • *give injections*

➤ Use the information about each job numbered below to practise
talking about job skills.

Sample Dialogue

Student A: I'm getting ready to look for work.
Student B: Can you tell me something about your job skills?
Student A: Well, I was a *nurse* in my country. I know how to *check vital signs* and I can *take blood pressure*.
Student B: Oh! Is that right? And do you know how to *give medication*?
Student A: Yes, I do. I can *give injections,* too.
Student B: That's good. It's very important to be able to describe what you can do.

1. hairdresser • cut and style hair
               • give perms
               • dye and highlight hair
               • ▬▬▬▬

2. mechanic   • check car engines
               • do auto body repairs
               • repair automatic transmissions
               • ▬▬▬▬

3. electrician • do commercial and
                 residential wiring
               • wire electrical panels
               • repair appliances
               • ▬▬▬▬

4. accountant • keep records
               • plan budgets
               • estimate costs
               • ▬▬▬▬

5. farmer   • plant crops
               • harvest crops
               • raise dairy cattle
               • ▬▬▬▬

YOUR TURN

➤ Practise the dialogue using your own job title and job skills.

 page 69 Do WB 5. Describing a Job   Categorizing Job Duties

Filling in a Registration Form for Employment Counselling

READING 3

WRITING

You can sometimes get help with your job search through an employment counselling agency. You may have to fill in a registration form. This will give the agency an idea about what your goals are. It will also tell them about your education, training and past work experience.

➤ Read a registration form with information about Wesson. This will help you prepare to fill out your own registration form.

➤ Practise filling out a form in the workbook.

Employment Counselling Agency Registration Form

Name: **Perez**   **Wesson**   **Roberto**   Birth date: **04/24/74**
　　　Surname　　　　First　　　Middle　　　　　　　　　　　m/d/y

Address: **987**　　　　　**Victoria Drive**
　　　　Number　　　　　　　Street

Vancouver　　　　　　　**British Columbia**　　　　**V7C 0Y0**
　　City　　　　　　　　　　　Province　　　　　　　Postal Code

Education:
What is your highest grade completed? 1 2 3 4 5 6 7 8 9 10 11 ⑫
Year completed **1992**

Type of school	Number of years	Name of certificate, degree or diploma	Year that you completed
College	Vancouver Community College	English for Medical Purposes	2004
University	University of Havana Cuba	Doctor of Veterinary Medicine	1998
Vocational or Trade	N/A		

Work History:
(Please begin with most recent job)

Company	From	To	Position	Salary or Wage	Reason for Leaving
Santiago Dairy Farms Cuba	2000	2002	Head Veterinarian	$25 per month (Can$)	Moved to Canada
Martinez Veterinary Clinic, Cuba	1998	2000	Assistant Veterinarian	$15 per month (Can$)	Job advancement New employer

Cont'd

Registration Form (continued)

1. State the type of job that you are looking for.

Veterinarian's Assistant

2. What other kind of work would you be willing to take?

Animal Welfare Assistant, Zookeeper's Assistant, Livestock Inspector

3. What salary range do you expect for these jobs?

The going rate*

4. What is the minimum starting wage that you are willing to accept?

$10.00 per hour

5. Which of the following types of work would you be willing to accept?

(Part-time)   Full-time   Shift work

6. How long have you been out of work?

18 months

7. How long have you been looking for work?

2 months

8. Do you have a resume? Yes X *No*____
   (If you have a resume, please provide a copy)

9. Which of the following do you want help with?

X Job leads and referrals   X Interview skills

____ Writing a resume   X Organizing a job search

* the usual rate of pay for a certain job

Tips for Filling out Forms

- Forms should be filled out accurately.
- Forms should be completed fully. Never leave empty spaces. Use N/A for items that don't apply to you.
- Educational information in a form should be supported with documents.
- Always print clearly in pen.

BEYOND THE CLASSROOM

➤ Check the Yellow Pages for employment assistance agencies.

➤ Collect registration forms and practise filling them out.

➤ Invite a speaker from one of the agencies to visit your classroom to speak about the services that are available.

 page 70 Do WB 6. Filling in a Registration Form for Employment Counselling

Getting Ready to Write a Resume

Jacqueline Castillo's job description includes a list of job responsibilities or duties. A list of your job responsibilities is important when you write a resume.

➤ Read Jacqueline Castillo's job description and one section of her resume.

➤ Complete the activity in your workbook.

Job Title: Job Placement Counsellor
Number of Years in Job: One year
Salary Range: $27,000 to $37,000

Jacqueline works at the Davis Job Placement Centre. She helps to match new Canadian professionals with local companies. Teachers, marketing consultants, accountants and mechanical engineers are some of the professionals she matches with local companies.

Her office assists approximately 300 people from all over the world. Clients learn Canadian methods of resume writing and job search techniques. Jacqueline needs to be able to promote her clients to employers.

Jacqueline Castillo

15 King Street
Toronto, Ontario
M3R 4T8
Phone: (416) 555-5372

WORK EXPERIENCE
2004 – 2005   **Job Placement Counsellor**
                Employment Skills Centre, Toronto

- Matching professionals with companies
- Assisting clients with resume writing
- Assisting clients with job search techniques
- Promoting clients to companies

---

 page 72 Do WB 7. Questions and Answers about Work

Cont'd

YOUR TURN

When you prepare a resume, you need to list the responsibilities you had in a previous job.

➤ In your notebook, write a list of your job responsibilities in your current or previous job.

FOCUS ON GRAMMAR

USING "BECAUSE OF"

Employers often ask you why you left your last job. You should be ready to answer this question.

Because of is followed by a noun or the *–ing* form of the verb (gerund).

> EXAMPLE: Counsellor: What was the reason for leaving your previous job?
>
> Wesson: It was just before I left my country. I left my job *because of <u>immigrating to Canada</u>*.

➤ Practise with a partner.

➤ Choose a reason for leaving a job from the Choice Box.

1. Employment counsellor: Could you explain why you left your last job?
   Maria: I hurt my back in a car accident and I was taking physiotherapy. I left my job because of ▓▓▓▓ .

2. Employment counsellor: Could I ask why you left your previous job?
   Mario: My wife had a baby and my company gave me a six-month leave to look after our child. I left my job because of ▓▓▓▓ .

3. Employment counsellor: What was the reason for leaving your former job?
   Khalil: Our company was getting smaller and closing some offices. They didn't need as many workers. I lost my job because of ▓▓▓▓ .

4. Employment counsellor: Please explain why you quit your last job.
   Sonia: I wanted to get a better job, so I needed more education and training. I left my job because of ▓▓▓▓ .

5. Employment counsellor: Do you mind telling me why you left your last job?
   Victor: My boss and I always had problems. I couldn't get along with her. We disagreed on many things. I left my job because of ▓▓▓▓ .

6. Employment counsellor: What was the reason for leaving your job?
   Wesson: My wife got transferred to a new job. She got a promotion. I left my job because of ▓▓▓▓ .

Choice Box

a personality conflict	my wife's transfer	my paternity leave
downsizing	a back injury	going back to school

YOUR TURN

If you had a previous job, why did you leave it?

➤ Share your answers with your classmates.

 page 73 Do WB 8. Using "Because of" to Give Reasons for Leaving a Job

 Giving Reasons for Leaving a Job

Skills and Preferences

 BREAKING IT DOWN

A skill is something you are good at. A preference is something you like doing.

Preference	Skill
I like animals.	I can solve problems easily.
I prefer working alone.	I know how to work on computers.
I enjoy helping people.	I am able to diagnose diseases.

➤ Read each of the sentences below.

➤ Decide if Wesson is talking about his skills or his preferences.

Wesson's Skills and Preferences

1. I like working with farm animals.
2. I can identify problems quickly.
3. I know how to diagnose diseases in animals.
4. I prefer working outside.
5. I enjoy working with computers in the clinic.
6. I can handle large farm animals.
7. I am able to follow instructions well.
8. I like having responsibility.

YOUR TURN

What skills do you have? What are your work preferences?

➤ Write a list in your notebook and share it with a partner.

 page 74 Do WB 9. Word Bank

Occupational Skills Game

 **CHECKING YOUR PROGRESS**

➤ Make cards that list the name of one occupation and three skills that go with each job. These occupation cards should reflect the occupations of people in your class. They can also include other occupations that interest you.

➤ Each student or player gets a dialogue card plus one occupation card.

➤ Now stand up and find a partner.

➤ Role-play the dialogue. Take turns being the job counsellor and the student.

➤ Then exchange occupation skill cards and look for a new partner.

➤ After you have been practising with several partners, try to say the dialogue without reading it. (Look at each other as you talk).

Dialogue Card

Job Counsellor:	What was your occupation ?
Client:	I was a ▨▨▨ in my previous job.
Job Counsellor:	Can you tell me something about your job skills?
Client:	I know how to ▨▨▨ and I can ▨▨▨ .
Job Counsellor:	Oh! Is that right? And do you know how to ▨▨▨ ?
Client:	Yes, I do.
Job Counsellor:	It's important to be able to describe what you can do.

Occupation Cards

An electrician can
- wire buildings.
- repair appliances.
- install circuit boxes.

A bartender can
- mix drinks.
- follow recipes.
- take orders.

A chef can
- plan menus.
- order food.
- organize and manage the kitchen and staff.

A hairdresser can
- cut and style hair.
- dye and highlight hair.
- sell hair products.

A taxi driver can
- read maps.
- follow directions.
- receive and give information.

An accountant can
- keep records.
- plan budgets.
- estimate costs.

 page 75 Do WB 10. Learning Progress Check

Applying for Work

Learning Opportunities

In this unit, you will have the opportunity to practise language skills that you will need to apply for work. You will learn:

- To greet someone and introduce yourself.
- To ask for assistance.
- To respond to an offer of assistance.
- To follow directions.
- To fill out a job application.
- To read job ads and postings.
- To write a cover letter.
- To read a graph or chart.

"How did you get your first job here?"

SETTING THE SCENE

When you are applying for a job, it is important to network and find places to apply. You need good skills to pick up, fill in and submit applications. You should know how to check back with the employer after they receive your application. It is important to understand the work culture in your new community.

Culture Note

Networking is a common way to find job openings.

TALKING IT OVER

1. Describe what you see in the picture.
2. What do you think the two men are discussing?
3. Why do you think Yasser is asking Victor this question?
4. How do you think Victor found his first job?

HOW ABOUT YOU?

1. Think about jobs that you have had. How did you get them?
2. How is looking for work different in your community?
3. Do people fill in applications in your community?

WORDS TO THINK ABOUT

1. to network
2. connections
3. to keep your eyes and ears open
4. to recommend someone
5. to apply for a job
6. to fill in an application form
7. It's tough.
8. to appreciate
9. job openings
10. to mention

Finding a Job

LISTENING

Listening for Key Information

➤ Listen carefully to the conversation between Yasser and Victor.

➤ Your teacher will play the dialogue in parts.

➤ Can you hear the *chunks of language* listed below?

➤ While listening, touch each chunk of language as you hear it. Notice how you can hear the new and important information by listening for the stress. The **stressed words** will be **longer, louder and slower** than the other words.

1. job openings
2. to apply for
3. so far
4. I don't really know
5. finding your first job
6. Canadian work experience
7. networked
8. tell everyone
9. keep their eyes and ears open
10. someone recommends
11. any other connections
12. work for
13. that would be great
14. I'll let you know
15. I'll also mention it
16. really appreciate your help

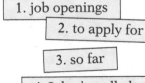 **page 76** Do WB 1. Listening for Key Information

Cont'd

Listening for Details

➤ Read the following questions. Think about what information you need to answer each question.

➤ Listen to the conversation. Write down one or two words in your notebook to answer each question.

➤ Share your answers with the class.

1. What does Victor ask Yasser?

2. What is Yasser worried about?

3. Why is finding a job in Canada tough?

4. How did Victor get his first job?

5. Who can Yasser ask to keep their eyes and ears open?

6. What kind of company does Victor work for?

7. What will Victor do to help Yasser?

YOUR TURN

➤ Work with a partner.

➤ Practise asking each other questions about Yasser and Victor.

➤ Use *chunks of language* for the answers.

 page 77 Do WB 2. Yasser Begins to Network

Listening for the Gist

Asking for Assistance and Offering Assistance

When you are looking for job openings, you might want to ask people for help.

➤ Think about ways that you could ask for help.

➤ Think about how people may offer to help you.

➤ Make a list of examples of asking for and offering assistance.

Do you know of any job openings?	→	Asking for assistance
I'll check at work for job openings.	→	Offering assistance

➤ Listen to the conversation.

➤ Decide if the person is asking for assistance or offering assistance.

 page 78 Do WB 3. Asking for Assistance and Offering Assistance

A Chart of the Hidden Job Market

Normally when we think of looking for work, we think about looking for advertised jobs. However, jobs are often not advertised. Employment services don't know about many of the new jobs either. They are not available through the traditional job-finding methods. You may need a little more help to look for jobs in different ways.

Sometimes, you can use charts to get information.

➤ Look at the pie chart to get the information to answer these questions.

➤ Discuss the answers with your classmates.

1. What are some ways of finding jobs?

2. How do most people find jobs?

3. What percentage (%) is the whole chart?

4. What percentage of job seekers finds a job through want ads?

5. What percentage of job seekers finds a job through informal job-seeking methods?

6. What is the difference between formal and informal job-seeking methods?

 **page 79** Do WB 4. Making a Pie Chart

The Hidden Job Market

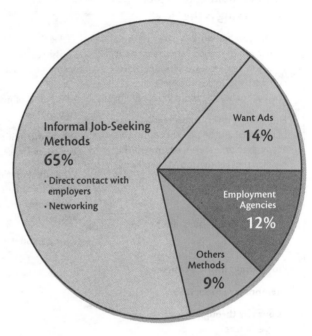

Robert Wegmann and Robert Chapman, *The Right Place at the Right Time: Finding a Job in the 1990s.* Ten Speed Press, 1990.

A Pamphlet about Networking

➤ First, read the questions below. Think about what kind of information you need to answer each question.

➤ Second, listen to your teacher read the pamphlet.

➤ Next, read the Networking Tips pamphlet with a partner.

➤ Finally, discuss the questions in a group and write the answers in your notebook.

1. What happens when you network?

2. What percentage of jobs is not advertised?

3. Why do you think that volunteer experience might be important?

Cont'd

4. What does a contact need to know about you?

5. What information can you get from a contact?

6. Who are some people that you will network with in the future?

NETWORKING TIPS

You are looking for a job. Networking is the "key."

When you network, you share and exchange information with others about your job search and skills. The more contacts you make, the more chances you have of hearing about job openings.

Networking is very important because between 60 and 80 percent of the jobs at any given time are not advertised. This is called the "Hidden Job Market." Some ways that people get their jobs are by:

- **Word of mouth (friends, neighbours, etc.)**

- **Walk-ins**

- **Job listings inside a company**

- **Temporary job services**

- **Contacts through volunteer experiences**

NETWORKING TIPS

Getting the word out to as many people as possible is very important. Make sure that your contact person knows:

- **What kind of position you are looking for**

- **What your skills and experience are**

- **What information you need (i.e., name of employers/ companies, phone numbers, addresses)**

- **Your personal information**

NETWORKING TIPS

Look over the list below and think about who you might contact. Make your own list and make a plan to contact them. Keep track of each contact, the dates you speak to him/her and the information you collect.

- **Family members**
- **Friends**
- **Classmates**
- **Counsellors**
- **Teachers**
- **Neighbours**
- **Former co-workers**
- **Workshop presenters**
- **Professional associations**
- **Someone at your place of worship**
- **Volunteer supervisors**
- **Employers**

YOUR TURN

➤ Think of all the people that you know.

➤ Make a list of people who might help you get information about job openings.

➤ How would you tell them that you are looking for a job? What questions would you ask?

➤ Remember to include classmates, friends, neighbours, former co-workers, family and people from your place of worship.

 page 79 Do WB 5. Using a Chart to Record Information

Abbreviations in Job Advertisements

WORD PLAY

When you read the want ads, you will see many abbreviations or short forms of words. People use abbreviations in classified ads to save space and money. Reading job ads can be confusing if you don't understand what these abbreviations mean. Luckily there are some rules.

Abbreviation Rules

1. Many abbreviations use the **first and last letters** of the word.	*wk. = week*
2. Some abbreviations use the **first few letters** of the word.	*mech. = mechanic*
3. Some abbreviations are made from the **first letter of each word.**	*DOT = Department of Transport*
4. Some abbreviations **leave out the vowels or consonants.**	*hrs. = hours*

➤ Read the following abbreviations you may find in job ads.

➤ Match the abbreviation with the meaning and write the answers in your notebook.

EXAMPLE: *1. p*

Vocabulary Strategy

If you don't understand a word, ask your teacher or look it up in your dictionary.

Abbreviation

1. wknds
2. min.
3. F/T
4. wtd
5. w/
6. req'd
7. cln crim. rec.
8. neg. wage
9. O/O
10. equip
11. exp'd
12. trk
13. hsehold
14. P/T
15. incl
16. refs.
17. co.
18. ASAP

Meaning

a) full-time
b) company
c) negotiate wage
d) required
e) as soon as possible
f) household
g) part-time
h) experienced
i) wanted
j) minimum
k) with
l) owner/operator
m) references
n) included
o) clean criminal record
p) weekends
q) truck
r) equipment

W. Cont'd

YOUR TURN

➤ Read the four abbreviation rules again.

➤ Pick out at least one example of each rule.

Job Advertisements

READING 3

The following ads are found in the job classifieds.

➤ Read the ads with a partner.

➤ Ask your teacher to help you with the new words.

➤ Look at the questions following the ads.

➤ Discuss the answers with your partner.

TRUCKING CLASS 1 DRIVER for Washington produce haul. Must be fluent in Eng. Be able to pass DOT drug test, cln crim. rec. & drivers abstract.* O/O also wtd w/ newer equip. Above average wages & home time. Fax resume & drivers abstract 604-546-1095

EXP'D BUSER/DELIVERY DRIVER req'd. Must have refs. Apply in person before 12 noon or betw'n 2-4 pm. 2790 Rupert.

CONSTRUCTION MULTI-TALENTED carpenter req'd w/own tools/trk. 604-970-8992

CREATIVE EXP'D COOK/ BAKER req'd for busy Bakery/Deli. Early mornings, wknds. P/T. Apply with resume to Carol's Fine Foods. Granville Island Market.

F/T HEATING & PLUMBING TECHNICIAN req'd for large Lower Mainland service co. Exp. in controls & maintenance req'd. Good wages, benefits and co. vehicle. Fax resume 604-433-4818

HOME SUPPORT WOMAN req'd as helper & companion, must be willing & able to do hsehold chores, long term in Port Moody area w/free time most days. Hrs 7pm-10am. Neg. wage incl rent, refs req'd 604-299-9876.

CERTIFIED MECHANIC. Must be able to work independently & do government inspections. Good wages for the right person. Call Stan 283-6541 or fax 283-6698.

HAIR STYLIST Min. 2 yrs exp. for Spirit Spa. Contact Mandy at 604-546-1397 or 604-477-1256.

LABOURER, Carpenter's helper & Carpenter req'd. Vehicle req'd, plus basic hand tools. Only reliable, hard-working individuals need apply. Must be available ASAP. 604-462-0760

Reading Strategy

To get important written details in a job ad, skim for the information. To skim, you look over the ad quickly to find specific information.

---

* A driver's abstract is a history of any accidents or demerits that a driver has on his/her record over a period of time.

Checking for Understanding

1. Which jobs say that the salary is good? What word means the same as salary?
2. Which jobs require experience?
3. Which job must you apply for in person?
4. Which job needs a worker as soon as possible?
5. Which job requires the worker to go out of the country?
6. Which job is a nighttime job?
7. Which job requires a drug screen? Why do you think it is important?
8. Which job has benefits? What benefits do you think are important?
9. Which job requires the worker to do government inspections?
10. Which jobs require the worker to have his own tools?
11. What is a "driver's abstract"? Which job requires that you have a good driver's abstract?
12. Which job would you like to apply for?

YOUR TURN

➤ On the Internet, go to www.google.ca and search for jobs under *Classifieds Canada*.

➤ Pick out three interesting jobs to share with the class.

 page 80 Do WB 6. Job Ads

USING INDEFINITE PRONOUNS

We use indefinite pronouns to talk about a person when we don't know who the person is exactly.

Some indefinite pronouns are:

somebody
someone   } a person but we don't know who it is
anybody
anyone

Rule	Example
Use **someone** or **somebody** to speak about people in a statement.	*I need to speak to **someone** about a job.*
Use **anyone** or **anybody** to speak about people in a negative.	*There isn't **anyone** available at the moment.*
Use **anyone, anybody, someone** or **somebody** in a question.	*Will **someone** be available at 9:00?* *Will **anyone** be available at 9:00?*

Yasser has been networking to find a job. Victor told him about a job opening. Yasser is picking up an application form.

➤ With a partner, read the following conversation out loud.

➤ As you read, fill in the missing indefinite pronouns. Sometimes, two answers are possible.

Twin Rivers
Construction Company

Christine Gerrard
Human Resources Officer

876 Silver Street, Kingston, Ontario
(613) 662-2010

EXAMPLE:	Can I speak to *someone* about the job you have advertised?
Yasser:	I'm here about the job opening. Is there ⬚⬚⬚ I can get an application from?
Receptionist:	Sure. Go to Human Resources on the second floor. There isn't ⬚⬚⬚ there right now, but there should be ⬚⬚⬚ in a few minutes. Just have a seat in the office. ⬚⬚⬚ will take care of you.
Yasser:	Is there ⬚⬚⬚ I should ask to speak to?
Receptionist:	Christine Gerrard is the person you need to speak to.

Yasser:	Hello Christine. My name is Yasser Mohammad. I'd like to apply for the job as a bricklayer. Do you have any application forms?
Christine:	Sure, here you go. How did you hear about the opening?
Yasser:	I spoke to ⬚⬚⬚ at my son's soccer game. I don't know if you know him. His name is Victor. He told me I should apply. That's how I found out.
Christine:	We like to hire ⬚⬚⬚ our employees recommend. They usually make good choices.
Yasser:	Is there ⬚⬚⬚ I can speak to when I drop off my application?
Christine:	I'll be able to answer most of your questions. Do you have time for a short interview now? I'll see if ⬚⬚⬚ is available. They're shorthanded right now.

Picking up Applications

SPEAKING

These conversations are examples of what you might say when you are picking up applications. They will help you to learn what is appropriate to say in Canadian culture.

➤ Read the model dialogue. Notice the use of indefinite pronouns.

➤ With a partner, role-play the dialogues for the following situations.

Model Dialogue

Job Seeker: Are you hiring anyone? I'm looking for work as a bricklayer.

Receptionist: Sorry, we aren't hiring anyone at the moment.

Job Seeker: Could I still get a job application, please?

Receptionist: Here you go.

Job Seeker: Is there someone I can contact for more information?

Receptionist: The manager would be someone you should speak with.

Job Seeker: Could I get a business card, please?

"Do you have any job openings?"

Situation 1

Job Seeker: Say that you are a bricklayer and you are looking for work. Ask if they have any openings.

Receptionist: Apologize. Say that they don't need anyone at this time.

Job Seeker: Ask for an application form anyway.

Receptionist: Give him/her an application and say "There you are."

Job Seeker: Ask if you can get the name of someone doing the hiring.

Receptionist: Tell him/her that the supervisor is the person to talk to.

Job Seeker: Ask if it is possible to speak to the supervisor now.

Situation 2

Job Seeker: Ask if they have any job openings for bricklayers.

Receptionist: Tell him/her that they will be looking for someone in the next week or two.

Job Seeker: Ask politely if you may have an application.

Receptionist: Give him/her an application. Say, "There you go."

Job Seeker: Ask if they could recommend someone that you could talk to.

Receptionist: Tell him/her to call the human resources officer. Say that she is usually here by 9:00.

Job Seeker: Ask if they mind if you wait for her.

Situation 3

Job Seeker: Say that you are currently looking for work. Ask if they are doing any hiring.

Receptionist: Tell him/her that they might be hiring someone later on.

Job Seeker: Ask if they mind if you pick up an application form.

Receptionist: Say, "This is what you need."

Job Seeker: Ask if you can get the name of the person doing the hiring.

Receptionist: Say that the boss is the best person to talk to.

Job Seeker: Ask if you can make an appointment.

Cont'd

BEYOND THE CLASSROOM

➤ Go out into the community and pick up job applications. »»

➤ Report to the class.

➤ What questions did you ask? What information did you get?

 Questions to Ask When You Pick up Job Applications

PRONUNCIATION POINTER

MORE LINKING

Linking Consonant + Vowel

We've looked at linking **consonant + vowel.** When a word ends in a single consonant and the next word begins with a vowel, the consonant sound links the two words.

EXAMPLES: *It's a great evening.*

Some jobs open up.

A list of employers

Pronunciation Hint ⟅

Understanding these rules will help you with both listening and pronunciation.

Linking Consonant to Consonant

When a word that ends with a stop consonant (b, d, g, k, p, t) is followed by a word that begins with a consonant, the stop consonant is usually not released. The tongue or lips move to the place to make the sound but then move immediately to make the next consonant sound in the next word.

➤ Listen to each short phrase.

➤ Repeat the phrase, focusing on the linking.

1. job search

2. Talk to him.

3. I heard that.

4. That sounds good.

5. an immediate job opening

6. I mentioned that.

7. the right thing

8. get help

9. employment counsellor

10. check my application

11. take breaks

12. eat well

13. my friend Victor

14. an enthusiastic person

Linking Identical Consonant Sounds

Sometimes, the consonant sound at the end of one word is the same as the beginning consonant sound of the next word. When this happens, the two consonants are usually pronounced as one long consonant.

➤ Listen and repeat these phrases to practise this kind of linking.

1. with thanks

2. I talked to friends

3. a clear reason

4. a serious student

5. a careful listener

6. a job bank

7. household duties

8. important to network

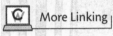 More Linking

Sections of Application Forms

 WORD PLAY

When you read an application form, you will see that there are different sections in it. The employer asks for many kinds of information. What are the sections of an application form? What information does the employer want in each section?

➤ Match the sections of the application form with the information an employer wants to know.

➤ Write the answers in your notebook.

EXAMPLE: *1. g*

Sections of an Application Form

1. Personal Information
2. Education and Training
3. Employment History
4. Skills
5. Employment Goals
6. References
7. Hobbies and Interests

What do employers want to know?

a) where, when and what courses you studied

b) things that you know how to do

c) your job plans now and in the future

d) people who will give the employer information about you

e) information about what jobs you have had

f) what things you like to do in your free time

g) your full name, address and phone number

 page 82 Do WB 7. Sections of an Application Form

Filling in an Application for Employment

READING 4

WRITING

➤ Read Yasser's employment application.

➤ Look at the different kinds of information that he needs to put on the application.

➤ Practise filling in an application in your workbook.

TWIN RIVERS CONSTRUCTION COMPANY

APPLICATION FOR EMPLOYMENT

Please Print. Fill out all sections of this application.

Name: **Akol** (LAST) **Yasser** (FIRST) **Ahmed** (MIDDLE)

Address: **1929 Birchwood Drive apt. 229**

City: **Kingston** Province: **ON** Postal Code: **K3P 5B7**

POSITION APPLIED FOR: **Bricklayer**

Date available to start: **April 26, 2005**

EDUCATIONAL HISTORY

Name of School	Location	Certificate/Diploma	Year Completed
Northern Vocational	Kartoum, Sudan	Heavy Duty Equipment Certificate	1995
Juba Trade College	Juba, Sudan	Certificate of Masonry	1994
Juba Central H.S.	Juba, Sudan	Grade 12 Diploma	1992

EMPLOYMENT HISTORY (List your previous employers beginning with the most recent)

Company: **Ontario Stone and Brick**   Supervisor's Name: **Steve Scheller**

Address: **4445 Heather Street, Detroit, MI**   Start and Leave Dates: **July 1999 – March 2004**

Phone: **(313) 252-9908**   Final Rate of Pay: **$18.50/hr.**

Position Held: **Bricklayer**   Reason for Leaving: **Laid off**

SKILLS (List skills, experience and equipment you can operate)

I have 5 years experience as a residential bricklayer. I have 2 years experience in block

basements and stucco masonry. I can operate heavy-duty machines and cement mixers.

I follow directions very well and enjoy working with construction crews.

REFERENCES (List people other than employers or relatives)

Name	Address	Telephone	Occupation	Years Known
Bruce Johnson	678 North Street	(313) 445-1234	Business owner	7

OTHER (Please check Yes or No to the following.)

Do you have your own vehicle?   Yes ☑ No ☐

Have you ever been convicted of an offence under the Criminal Code of Canada?   Yes ☐ No ☑

Do you have any illness or physical limitations?   Yes ☐ No ☑

If yes, please explain: ___N/A_____

Are you willing to work overtime and weekends?   Yes ☑ No ☐

I declare that the information given by me in this application is true and complete.

I understand that if I am employed, false statements on this application shall be sufficient cause for dismissal.

In connection with my application, I give consent to Twin Rivers to make inquiries to verify all information.

_____ *Yasser Akol* _____   April 5, 2005
Signature   Date

FOR OFFICE USE ONLY

Position: _____

S.I.N. _____

Interviewed by: _____

Date: _____**Starting Date:** _____

Starting Rate: _____

FOR OFFICE USE ONLY

📖 **page 83** Do WB 8. Filling in a Job Application Form

A Cover Letter

READING 5

WRITING

Whenever you send an application and/or a resume, you also need to send a cover letter. A cover letter introduces you to the employer and may help you get an interview.

➤ Read Yasser's cover letter to Twin Rivers Construction Company.

➤ Discuss the answers to the questions with a partner.

➤ Practise writing your own cover letter in your workbook.

Cont'd

YASSER AKOL
229-1929 Birchwood Drive
Kingston, ON
K3P 5B7
(613) 995-5432

April 5, 2005
Mr. R. L. Collins
Twin Rivers Construction Company
876 Silver St.
Kingston, ON
M5L 2G5

Dear Mr. Collins,

I would like to apply for the position of bricklayer. I heard about this opening from your employee, Victor Lopez.

I have many years experience as a bricklayer in the U.S. I also worked as a bricklayer in my native country, Sudan. I am a skilled and independent worker.

I have enclosed an application and a resume. They describe my experience and skills.

I would appreciate the opportunity to meet with you about the bricklayer position.

You can call me at home after 4:00 p.m. or contact me by e-mail: yaakol@yahoo.com

Thank you for considering my letter of application.

Sincerely,

Yasser Akol

Yasser Akol

Checking for Understanding

➤ Look at the letter and find where:

1. Yasser greets the employer in the letter.
2. He tells how he heard about the job.
3. He tells the position he is applying for.
4. He says he has a lot of experience as a bricklayer.
5. He tells what he has enclosed in the envelope.
6. He asks for an interview.
7. He tells the employer how he can contact him.
8. He thanks the employer for looking at this application.
9. He ends his letter politely.

 **page 84** Do WB 9. Writing a Cover Letter

USING ADVERBS AND ADJECTIVES TO DESCRIBE

When Yasser was filling out job application forms and beginning his job search, he learned some important information about Canadian culture.

Don't leave any empty blanks on a job application form. Fill in all blanks **completely***.*

Adjectives	Adverbs
An adjective is a word that describes a noun/pronoun.	An adverb is a word that describes a verb.
Words we know as adjectives become adverbs by adding **ly**.	
She is **neat** in her work. She is a **neat** printer. He is **careful** when he fills in forms.	She prints **neatly.** He fills in the form **carefully.**
Fast, hard, early and **late** can be adjectives or adverbs. The adjective **good** changes to **well** as an adverb.	
Carol is a **good** speller.	Carol spells **well.**

➤ Work with a partner.

➤ Read each sentence and then change the adjective in **bold** to an adverb.

➤ Write your answers in your notebook.

➤ Your answers will help you when filling out forms and looking for jobs.

EXAMPLE:
Gert is a **careful** reader.
Gert reads application forms *carefully.*

Spelling Strategy
If you have difficulty spelling these adverbs, check them in your dictionary.

1. Laurie is a **neat** printer.
   Laurie prints ▢▢▢▢▢ on her application.

2. Stephen is **truthful** when he answers questions on application forms.
   Stephen answers the questions ▢▢▢▢▢.

3. Karin is a **perfect** speller.
   Karin spells words ▢▢▢▢▢.

4. Grant is **serious** about looking for a job.
   Grant is looking for a job ▢▢▢▢▢.

5. Mary Jean is a **good** organizer.
   She organizes her job search ▢▢▢▢▢.

6. Kathy has **legible** handwriting.
   She writes ▢▢▢▢▢ on her applications.

7. Linda is a **positive** thinker.
   She thinks ▢▢▢▢▢ about her job search.

8. Anders is a **confident** speaker.
   When he asks for an application, he speaks ▢▢▢▢▢.

9. Andrea can give a **clear** explanation of her goals.
   She can explain her goals ▢▢▢▢▢.

10. John is **realistic** about his job prospects.
    He evaluates his situation ▨▨▨▨▨▨ .

11. The employer made a **quick** assessment of the applicant.
    The employer assessed the applicant ▨▨▨▨▨▨ .

12. Christine has an **immediate** job opening.
    She is willing to hire someone ▨▨▨▨▨▨ .

13. Evan is an **enthusiastic** person.
    He applies for jobs ▨▨▨▨▨▨ .

14. Brian is an **effective** planner.
    He plans his job search ▨▨▨▨▨▨ .

 page 86 Do WB 10. Describing How People Do Things

 Personal Qualities

Ways to Stay Positive

READING 6

➤ Read this extract from a magazine article.

Finding a job can take weeks or months. Job seekers often feel angry, upset and depressed. Sometimes, they want to give up. Brochures and pamphlets sometimes have information about how job seekers can stay positive. Practise reading this kind of information and get some ideas about how to stay positive during your job search.

1. Get help from people who can give you emotional support.

2. Get help from someone who can give you professional support.

3. Take care of your health. Eat well and exercise.

4. Continue to learn, get experience and improve your skills.

5. Take breaks from your job search and reward yourself.

6. Plan your job search carefully and stay organized.

Things I Would Do to Stay Positive

➤ Think about how you would use the suggestions from the list above to help you stay positive.

➤ Look at the list that Yasser wrote. Use his list to get ideas.

➤ Share your ideas with your classmates.

➤ Write your list in your notebook. Use it to help you stay positive when you are applying for work.

Yasser's List

1. I'd get help from my friend, Victor.

2. I'd contact an employment counsellor.

3. I'd get lots of exercise and eat well.

4. I'd continue my English class to improve my pronunciation.

5. I'd buy tickets to go to a professional soccer game with Victor.

6. I'd make a list of employers that I have contacted. I would call them back and check on my application.

BEYOND THE CLASSROOM

➤ Contact agencies for job seekers.

➤ Look for brochures and pamphlets that have information on ways to stay positive.

 **page 87** Do WB 11. Speaking Positively

 Thinking Positively

Picking up Applications

When you apply for work, you will use language to do many things. Look at the language functions in the box. You can use functions like these when you go to pick up applications.

Action	→ Language Function
We start a conversation.	Opening a conversation
We tell someone our name.	Introducing oneself
We ask for help.	Asking for assistance
We say that we will help.	Offering assistance
We tell someone how to do something.	Giving directions
We end a conversation.	Closing a conversation

➤ Read the sentences below. Think about what the speaker is doing.

➤ Look at the list of language functions.

➤ Choose the function to describe the language in each sentence.

➤ Discuss your answers with the class.

EXAMPLE: *1. f*

We say

1. Thank you. You have been very helpful.

2. How can I help you?

3. I'm looking for work. Do you have any openings?

4. Take this application. Fill it in and drop it off by the end of the week.

5. My name is Yasser Mohammed.

6. Hello. How are you today?

Language Functions

a) Offering assistance

b) Asking for assistance

c) Introducing oneself

d) Opening a conversation

e) Giving directions

f) Closing a conversation

YOUR TURN

➤ Work in a group.

➤ Think of more ways you would use language to offer assistance, ask for assistance, introduce yourself, open a conversation, give directions and close a conversation.

➤ Write your answers on the board to share with the class.

page 88 Do WB 12. Picking up Applications

Networking to Find a Job

CHECKING YOUR PROGRESS

➤ Work with a partner.

➤ Practise the language you would use to find a job.

➤ Present a dialogue to your class.

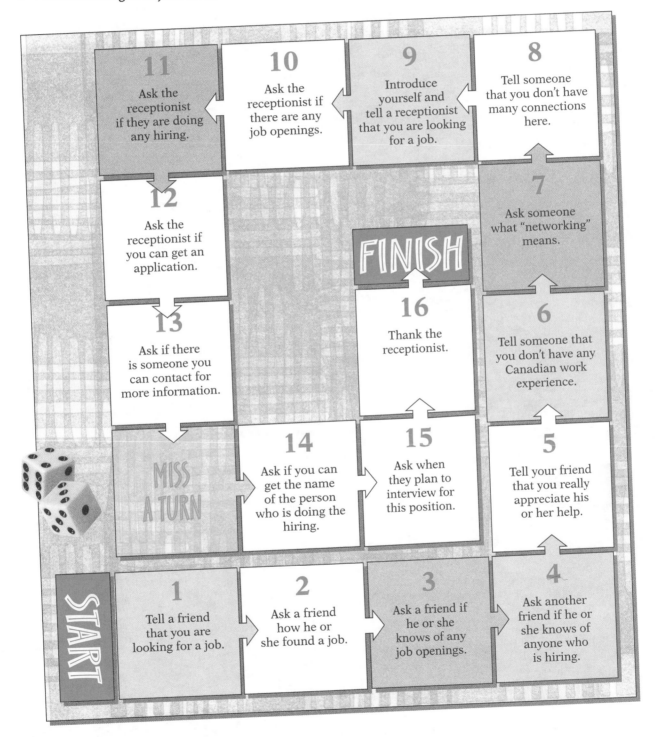

11
Ask the receptionist if they are doing any hiring.

10
Ask the receptionist if there are any job openings.

9
Introduce yourself and tell a receptionist that you are looking for a job.

8
Tell someone that you don't have many connections here.

12
Ask the receptionist if you can get an application.

7
Ask someone what "networking" means.

13
Ask if there is someone you can contact for more information.

FINISH

16
Thank the receptionist.

6
Tell someone that you don't have any Canadian work experience.

MISS A TURN

14
Ask if you can get the name of the person who is doing the hiring.

15
Ask when they plan to interview for this position.

5
Tell your friend that you really appreciate his or her help.

START

1
Tell a friend that you are looking for a job.

2
Ask a friend how he or she found a job.

3
Ask a friend if he or she knows of any job openings.

4
Ask another friend if he or she knows of anyone who is hiring.

page 89 Do WB 13. Word Bank | **page 90** Do WB 14. Learning Progress Check

Lifelong Learning

Learning Opportunities

Do you like to learn? Do you like to keep on learning how to do new things? Do you have the language skills to get information about programs and classes? Do you know about lifelong learning opportunities in your community? In this unit, you will learn:

- To talk about your immediate plans.
- To talk about your feelings.
- To follow directions.
- To read a community activity guide.
- To record important information from a guide.
- To describe a learning experience.
- To write a personal message.

St. Francis Recreation Centre
Community Activity Courses

Come out and meet your neighbour

Learn a new skill or hobby

Childcare available

Lifelong learning opportunities

SETTING THE SCENE

When you register for courses or programs, you need to understand the staff and instructors. You may want to talk to someone about your plans. There are often community activity guides that you can read to get information.

Culture Note

Community clubs, schools, universities and colleges often offer many different courses and programs in the evenings and on weekends to encourage lifelong learning.

TALKING IT OVER

1. Describe what you see in the picture of the two women.

2. What information do you think will be in a community activity guide?

3. What courses do you think the women might take?

HOW ABOUT YOU?

1. Do you have a hobby or special interest?

2. Have you ever taken an evening course?

3. Where do adults go to take evening courses in your community?

WORDS TO THINK ABOUT

1. lifelong learning
2. to register
3. courses
4. skill
5. hobby
6. recreation centre
7. activity guides
8. leisure programs
9. arts and crafts

Talking about Courses

 LISTENING

Listening for Key Information

➤ Listen carefully to the conversation between Sina and her neighbour, Maria.

➤ Your teacher will play the dialogue in parts.

➤ Can you hear the *chunks of language* listed below?

➤ While listening, touch each chunk of language as you hear it. Notice the use of idiomatic expressions. You will hear these expressions used in everyday language.

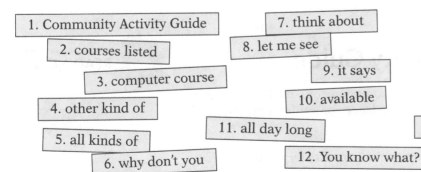

1. Community Activity Guide
2. courses listed
3. computer course
4. other kind of
5. all kinds of
6. why don't you
7. think about
8. let me see
9. it says
10. available
11. all day long
12. You know what?
13. do something for yourself
14. I know but
15. on the same night
16. give you a ride

 page 91 Do WB 1. Listening for Key Information

Cont'd

Listening for Details

➤ Read the following questions. Think about what information you need to answer each question.

➤ Listen to the dialogue. Write down one or two words to answer each question.

➤ Discuss your answers.

1. Where do the two women meet?
2. What information is in the Community Activity Guide?
3. Do they offer arts and crafts courses?
4. How many chairs does Maria need to re-cover?
5. What word means the same as reupholstering?
6. Why is it difficult for Maria to take a course?
7. Is babysitting available at the courses?
8. How can Sina help Maria?

Culture Note

Did you know you can pick up a community activity guide free of charge at your local library or fitness centre? Sometimes the guides are delivered with the newspapers or dropped into you mailbox with other flyers. Keep an eye out for this important booklet.

Listening for the Gist

What's the Message?

When we register for a course or a program, we may get a voice mail message on the phone about our registration. The message will tell us if we can attend or not.

This is a message for Paulo. I am sorry but the CPR class is now full.	→ Paulo cannot attend.
I would like to leave a message for Sina. Please come to 200 Main Street next Monday for your first computer class.	→ Sina can attend.

➤ Listen to each phone message. Does the message tell the person that they can attend or not?

➤ Discuss your choices with your classmates.

Culture Note

If your course is cancelled, you will get a refund.

 page 92 Do WB 2. What's the Message?

A Community Activity Guide      READING 1

Many people like to take community or recreation courses. It's an opportunity to get out of a normal routine and to experience something new, especially during the winter.

➤ Read the following information from a community activity guide.

➤ Match the description of each course with one of the course titles.

➤ Write the answers in your notebook.

EXAMPLE: *3. A*

Community Services Department

Activity Guide for Fun & Educational Programs – St. Francis Recreation Centre

Our goal is to help neighbours meet each other and learn together. We help people develop a feeling of community.

A. Learn how to cook recipes for your diabetic that the whole family will enjoy. Learn to make great tasting food that follows the dietary guidelines for people with diabetes.
Fee $55.00   6 weeks   Mon. 7:00 - 9:00
Start Jan. 5

B. Learn the proper use of basic hand and power tools. You will work on two projects with wood. You can buy the supplies at the course.
Fee $ 55.00   8 weeks   Wed. 6:30 - 9:00
Start Jan. 7

C. Have you bought a new digital camera? Do you want to learn how to use it? This course is for you! Learn camera basics. Bring your camera.
Fee $30.00   3 weeks   Thurs. 7:00 - 9:00
Start Jan. 8

D. A beginner's program for people wanting to learn to play one of Canada's most popular sports. This program teaches rules, etiquette and strategy. Please bring a curling broom, clean, flat footwear and a slider.
Fee $66.00   6 weeks   Wed. 7:00 - 9:00
Start Jan. 7

E. Would you like to be prepared to help in an emergency such as a heart attack or choking? Do you require First Aid training for a job? The Red Cross will teach this course.
Fee $35.00   1 day   Thurs. 7:00 - 9:00
Start Jan. 8

F. Learn the step-by-step of reupholstering through demonstration and by doing your own project. Bring a chair to be re-covered in class. We have no storage.
Fee $70.00   6 weeks   Tues. 6:00 - 8:00
Start Jan. 6

G. This program is for skaters of all levels, ages and abilities. Learn or improve your skills in skating. Enjoy professional instruction where families can learn together at their own rate. Bring your skates and a helmet.
Fee $55.00   10 weeks   Mon. 6:30 - 7:30
Start Jan. 5

H. Do you want to learn how to use a computer? Well, here's your chance. Skills start from turning on the computer. No previous knowledge is needed. You work your way through the workshops on your own computer and at your own speed. Enrolment is limited. Bring $10.00 to the first class for a student manual.
Fee $85.00   10 weeks   Tues. 6:00 - 8:00
Start Jan. 6

Babysitting available. Call Jan at 669-5128.

Course Titles

1. Basic Woodworking
2. Digital Photography
3. Cooking for Diabetics
4. Family Skating Instruction
5. CPR/First Aid
6. Introduction to Computers
7. Furniture Reupholstery
8. Learn to Curl

Reading Strategy

To read short texts, use key words to get the gist or main idea.

YOUR TURN

Discuss with your partner.

➤ Which course interests you?

➤ Can you think of a different community course that you would like to take?

 page 92 Do WB 3. Recording Information from a Guide

What Kind of Program Is It?

The goal of the Community Services Department is to provide safe, healthy and interesting programs for all participants. Do you want to learn a new skill? Are you interested in playing a team sport? Do you want to join a fitness class? Do you have a hobby? Would you like to learn how to do arts and crafts?

When you read a recreation guide, you will see a number of general program headings in the table of contents like the ones below.

Program Headings

1. Do-It-Yourself Around the Home
2. Arts, Crafts and Hobbies

3. Active Living and Fitness
4. Team Sports

➤ Write the four program headings in your notebooks.

➤ Read the list of sixteen class titles.

➤ Work with a partner and discuss the program types and class titles. Discuss what you might do in the different classes.

➤ Write the class title under the appropriate program heading.

EXAMPLE: *Team Sports*
    Basketball

Class Titles

a) Learn to Knit

b) Indoor Soccer

c) Aqua Fitness

d) Basic Car Maintenance

e) Beadwork on Moccasins

f) Basketball

g) Curling

h) Yoga

i) Stretch and Strengthen

j) Reupholster Your Furniture

k) Paint and Paper Your Walls

l) Floor Hockey

m) Introduction to Pottery

n) Water Colour Painting Level 1

o) Ballroom Dancing – Beginner

p) Woodworking – Build a Bookcase

BEYOND THE CLASSROOM

➤ Find an activity guide in your community.

➤ Find out what courses are offered under the program headings on this page.

 Finding Information in a Leisure Guide

Describing Our Feelings

Throughout our lives, situations change from time to time. We experience
different feelings. Some feelings are positive. Some feelings are negative.
We need language skills to talk about how we feel.

➤ Read each situation.

➤ Think about how each person would describe their feelings.

➤ Choose your answer from the Word Box below. Write your answer in
your notebook.

➤ When you finish, work with a partner to classify the feelings. Which feelings are
positive and which feelings are negative? Make two lists.

➤ Can you think of other words to describe feelings?

EXAMPLE: Maria is at home all day with young children. She's very lonely.
She doesn't see or talk to many adults. It's a depressing
situation. How does she describe her feelings? Maria says,
"I am _depressed_."

1. Paulo has a 65-year-old father with a bad heart. He calls his father from
work several times a day. How does he describe his feelings?
He says, "I am ▨▨▨▨▨."

2. Sina doesn't like her job. It's boring. She does the same thing day after
day. How does she describe her feelings? She says, "I am ▨▨▨▨▨."

3. Susan's husband has diabetes. She can't find many recipes with
ingredients her husband can eat. It is frustrating. How does she
describe her feelings? She says, "I am ▨▨▨▨▨."

4. Gurmeet is happy about winter coming. She wants to learn a winter
sport. She has never seen snow before! How does she describe
her feelings? She says, "I am ▨▨▨▨▨."

5. James thinks about his family and old friends a lot.
He misses his country very much. How does he describe
his feelings? He says, "I am ▨▨▨▨▨."

Word Box

excited	worried
frustrated	bored
homesick	depressed

YOUR TURN

Is it important to talk about your feelings? Who can you talk to?

➤ Share some ideas with your partner.

 page 93 Do WB 4. Describing Our Feelings

USING WANT AND NEED TO TALK ABOUT PLANS

We use **want** when we talk about things we would like to have. **Need** has a meaning of necessity. **Want** and **need** can be followed by a noun or an infinitive. **Need** has a stronger meaning than want.

You **want to** take a swimming class.

You **need to** have a bathing suit. You can't go into the swimming pool without a bathing suit.

Want and **need** follow the same rules.

	+ Noun	+ Infinitive
Need	Newcomers **need English.**	Newcomers **need to learn** English.
Want	He **wants** a **volunteer** to help him with his English.	He **wants to speak** English with a volunteer.

PART A

➤ Think of some things that you **need.**

➤ Think of some things that you **want.**

➤ Use the chart above to help you.

➤ Write two or three examples in your notebook.

PART B

➤ Work with a partner and use the prompts below to practise **want** and **need.**

EXAMPLE:

Student A: *What course does Gurmeet want to take?*

Student B: *She wants to take Learn to Curl.*

Student A: *What does she need?*

Student B: *She needs a curling broom and a slider.*

Ask his/her name	Ask what course he/she wants to take	Ask what he/she needs
1. Gurmeet (F)	Learn to Curl	A curling broom and a slider.
2. Ahmed (M)	Ballroom Dancing	A partner.
3. Yong (M)	Water Colour Painting Level 1	A $10 lab fee payable the first night.
4. Salvador (M)	Stretch and Strengthen	Gym clothes and runners required.
5. Paulo (M)	CPR	No equipment is necessary.
6. Violeta (F)	Digital Photography	A digital camera.
7. James (M)	Woodworking	Money to buy supplies at courses.
8. Sina (F)	Introduction to Computers	Bring a floppy disk to save work.
9. Susan (F)	Cooking for Diabetics	Bring a container with a lid to class.
10. Maria (F)	Furniture Reupholstery	Bring a chair.

Abbreviation note: F = female name; M = male name

BEYOND THE CLASSROOM

➤ Look at a leisure guide you have picked up in your community.

➤ Find three courses that you might take. What is the name of each course? What do you need for each course?

 page 94 Do WB 5. Using Want and Need to Talk about Plans

 Talking about Our Feelings and Future Plans

A Receipt

 READING 2

When you register for a course or program, you will receive information about your registration. Sometimes, you will get a receipt. The receipt shows that you paid for the course. It can also have information for you. Sometimes, you need to take it with you to your first class.

Paulo registered for a computer class.

➤ Read Paulo's receipt.

➤ Answer the questions that follow the text.

Date	Cash	Cheque	Amount	Name	Course	Starting Date	Time	Day	Phone
Sept. 13	✔		$50.00	Paulo Santos	Intro to Computers	Sept. 20	7:00–9:00	Monday	224-1221

Location: St. Francis High School

Receipt No. 098543
City of St. Francis
Community Services Dept.
224-7886

(Please show this receipt to the instructor at the first class.)

Checking for Understanding

➤ Can you read the receipt to get important information?

➤ Write the answers to the questions in your notebook.

1. What course is Paulo going to take?
2. How much did Paulo pay for his course?
3. Did he pay by cheque?
4. When does the course start?
5. How many days a week does Paulo go to the class?
6. How long does each class last?
7. Should Paulo keep the receipt? Why or why not?
8. What other information do you see on the receipt?

 page 95 Do WB 6. Reading a Receipt

BLENDED SOUNDS

When two sounds come together in speech, they often change to a different or blended sound.

Rule for Blended Sounds

When the sounds made by the letters *t, d, s* and *z* are followed by a /y/ sound in an unstressed syllable, the two sounds combine together to form a new sound.

Pronunciation Hint

Blended sounds are unstressed. The blending of syllables is natural and appropriate for native speakers.

PART A

➤ Listen to the sentences in the chart below.

➤ Then practise. Listen to the sentences again.

➤ Repeat after the model, paying attention to the palatalized or blended forms.

Write like this	Letters	Say like this
1. Where did‿you take the painting class?	d + y	Where /didja/* take the painting class?
2. What did‿you study last year?		What /didja/* study last year?
3. Did‿you know that babysitting is available?		/Didja/* know that babysitting is available?
4. Would‿you like to learn CPR?		/Wudja/* like to learn CPR?
5. I appreciate‿your kindness.	t + y	I appreciate /chor/* kindness.
6. Can you talk about‿your plans?		Can you talk /abouchor/* plans?
7. Why don't‿you think about taking a course?		Why /donchu/* think about taking a course?
8. Don't forget‿your money for a computer manual.		Don't /forgechor/* money for a computer manual.
9. What course interests‿you?	s + y	What course /intereshu/*?
10. Who takes‿you to class?		Who /takeshu/* to class?
11. Which friend picks‿you up?		Which friend /pickshu/* up?
12. Who helps‿you with your school work?		Who /helpshu/* with your school work?
13. Here's‿your chance.	z +y	/Herzhor/* chance.
14. Where's‿your computer class?		/Wherzhor/* computer class?
15. Who's‿your teacher?		/Whozhor/* teacher?
16. What's‿your plan?		/Whazhor/* plan?

*This is what it would sound like.

PART B

➤ Complete the following sentences with your own words.

➤ Practise saying each sentence to your partner.

1. I appreciate your ▭ .
2. Can you tell me about your ▭ ?
3. Why don't you ▭ ?
4. Don't forget your ▭ .
5. What interests you?
6. Who takes you ▭ ?

7. Who helps you ▭ ?
8. Where's your ▭ ?
9. Who's your ▭ ?
10. What's your ▭ ?
11. Did you know ▭ ?
12. Would you ▭ ?

YOUR TURN

➤ Choose three of the sentence starters that you could use with your friends or family.

➤ Share these with the class.

Blending Words

A Thank-You Note

READING 3

WRITING

Knowing how to write a thank-you note is very important. People write thank-you notes for a variety of reasons such as receiving gifts and getting help. Maria wants to thank Sina for the rides to her class every week.

➤ Read Maria's thank-you note.

➤ Discuss the questions below with a partner.

➤ Then write your own thank-you note.

Writing Strategy

*Remember! Capitalize days, months and names.
Capitalize the first word in the sentence.*

February 20, 2005

Dear Sina,

    I want to thank you for giving me a ride to my reupholstery class every Monday. I really liked the class and I learned a lot of new things. It was fun to meet new people. It was good to have some time out of the house. I also enjoyed chatting with you on the way to our classes.

    I appreciate your kindness and friendship. Thanks again.

Sincerely,

Maria

Cont'd

Checking for Understanding

➤ Discuss these questions with your classmates.

1. Who received this thank-you note?

2. Why did Maria write this note?

3. How did Maria feel about the class? Explain your answer.

4. Can you think of a different way she could say thank you?

5. How many times does Maria say thank you? What does she say each time?

 page 96 Do WB 7. Writing a Thank-You Note

[C] Writing a Letter to Request a Refund

Plans and Feelings

 BREAKING IT DOWN

When we talk about lifelong learning, we often talk about our plans and feelings.

Action	→ Language Function
We tell someone how we feel.	Expressing our feelings
We talk about our plans for the future.	Expressing future plans

➤ Look at the sentences below. Think about what the speaker is doing.

➤ Look at the language functions that you practised in this unit.

➤ Match the sentences with the correct function. Write the answers in your notebook.

EXAMPLE: *1. b*

We say

1. I'm going to take a cooking course.

2. I'm bored with my job.

3. I plan to learn how to speak Spanish.

4. I'm tired of staying home all day.

5. I want to find a computer course to improve my skills.

6. I'm so lonely. I don't have any friends.

7. My plans are to learn how to skate.

Language Functions

a) Expressing feelings

b) Expressing future plans

page 97 Do WB 8. Positive and Negative Feelings

Taking a Course

➤ Work with a partner. Practise the kind of language that you might use when you take a course or program.

➤ Write what you would say in each situation.

➤ When you finish, you will have a dialogue between two friends. One is asking for information about a class and the other is sharing information.

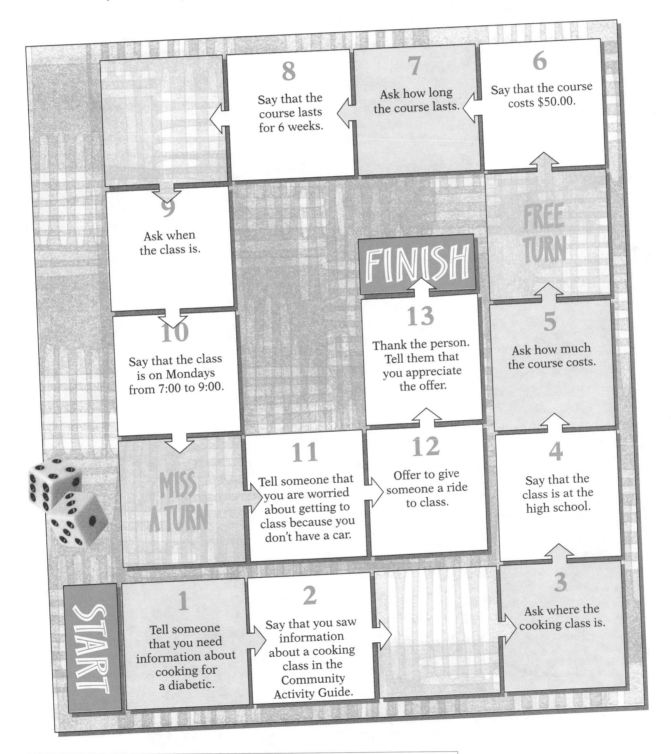

8 Say that the course lasts for 6 weeks.

7 Ask how long the course lasts.

6 Say that the course costs $50.00.

9 Ask when the class is.

FREE TURN

FINISH

13 Thank the person. Tell them that you appreciate the offer.

5 Ask how much the course costs.

10 Say that the class is on Mondays from 7:00 to 9:00.

MISS A TURN

11 Tell someone that you are worried about getting to class because you don't have a car.

12 Offer to give someone a ride to class.

4 Say that the class is at the high school.

START

1 Tell someone that you need information about cooking for a diabetic.

2 Say that you saw information about a cooking class in the Community Activity Guide.

3 Ask where the cooking class is.

page 98 Do WB 9. Word Bank   **page 99** Do WB 10. Learning Progress Check

Getting Ready
for a Job Interview

Learning Opportunities

Can you use the language you have learned in the previous units? In this unit, you will take part in a role-playing activity. There are two roles: job applicant and job interviewer. You will have the chance to play both roles. You will work in groups and practise the language you need to communicate in a real job interview.

As you work through the role-play, you will review how :

- To begin and end a conversation.
- To recognize and use stress and intonation in conversation.
- To read and follow instructions.
- To express future plans.
- To fill in a form.
- To listen and respond to questions.
- To ask for an explanation.
- To describe skills and abilities.
- To describe employment goals.
- To talk about occupations and work experience.
- To prepare a resume.
- To read job ads and postings.
- To write a simple business memo.

Follow ten steps to complete the role-playing activity. The goal of the role-play is to choose the most appropriate candidate for a job.

STEP 1 FORM A GROUP.

➤ Form an initial group of six students.

➤ Name your group A, B, C and so on.

➤ Within the group, form two smaller sub-groups of three students.

EXAMPLE: A1 and A2.

Group A		Group B		Group C		Group D	
A1	A2	B1	B2	C1	C2	D1	D2
👥👥👥	👥👥👥	👥👥👥	👥👥👥	👥👥👥	👥👥👥	👥👥👥	👥👥👥

STEP 2 CHOOSE A JOB ADVERTISEMENT.

You will learn new vocabulary about each job ad.

➤ Read the first job ad once. Make a list of words you don't know. Discuss these words in class. Then do the exercise for advertisement A1 in your workbook.

➤ Follow the same steps for each job ad.

 page 100 Do WB 1. Vocabulary in Job Ads

Job Advertisements

 **READING 1**

➤ Read your assigned job advertisement.

Reading Strategy

To understand difficult words, use a dictionary or ask a teammate or your teacher for help.

Group A

A1

Private Primary School located in quiet neighbourhood requires experienced ENGLISH TEACHER immediately for part-time position.

Must have 2 years experience and 2 job references. Must be patient, hard working, well prepared and dynamic. Teaching diploma in primary education. Bilingual.

A2

Maplewood School Commission is looking for a full-time LIBRARIAN.

The applicant should have a university degree in library science. The person should be comfortable with both adults and children. Computer skills are necessary. Ability to read French is important.

Group B

B1

West Centre is hiring a COMMUNITY CENTRE DIRECTOR.

Candidate must:
• have a college diploma in communications;
• have experience in planning and organizing educational programs for all ages;
• be responsible, creative and a team player;
• be fluent in English and oral French.

B2

Waterdown Medical Clinic is looking for a full-time DOCTOR'S RECEPTIONIST.

To qualify, you must have good secretarial and telephone skills and knowledge of family doctor/walk-in clinic procedures. You must also have basic computer knowledge. High level of fluency in English, both oral and written, is necessary. Good oral French is a plus.

Cont'd

Group C

C1

The municipality of Forest Park is presently seeking a professionally trained PARAMEDIC.

The candidate should have 2 years experience in the position. Must have excellent communication skills and knowledge of emergency situations related to Ambulance, Fire and Police services. Must be ready to work flexible hours. Knowledge of oral French is necessary.

C2

Port Avenue SuperMart is seeking a bilingual STORE CLERK.

The successful candidate must
- have a high school diploma;
- be honest and motivated;
- be polite with customers;
- be ready to work day and night shifts.

There is a possibility for advancement in the company.

Group D

D1

Smith, Trudeau and Clark is looking for an ASSISTANT ACCOUNTANT with experience in bookkeeping for small businesses.

Must have knowledge of computers and accounting software. A university degree in business is required. Must be fluent in English and French.

D2

Davidson Electronics needs an experienced in-store SALES PERSON.

The qualified candidate should have at least one year of experience in retail sales. Must be able to interact well with customers. Applicant will receive salary plus commission; must be highly motivated and a strong communicator. Computer skills are an advantage.

 Vocabulary in Job Ads

STEP 3 PREPARE FOR THE ROLE OF JOB APPLICANT.

➤ Read your assigned job advertisement again. Think about what each job requires. (See pages 155–156, Step 2)

EXAMPLE: Group A1 re-reads advertisement A1.
Group A2 re-reads advertisement A2.

➤ Read Pegah's resume on page 157.

➤ Prepare a resume to fit the job ad. Look at what the job requires. Prepare a resume for someone with that kind of experience.

 page 103 Do WB 2. Resume Worksheet

Group A		Group B		Group C		Group D	
A1	A2	B1	B2	C1	C2	D1	D2
Read ad A1. Prepare a resume.	Read ad A2. Prepare a resume.	Read ad B1. Prepare a resume.	Read ad B2. Prepare a resume.	Read ad C1. Prepare a resume.	Read ad C2. Prepare a resume.	Read ad D1. Prepare a resume.	Read ad D2. Prepare a resume.

Pegah's Resume

READING 2

Pegah recently applied for a teaching job at a high school. First, she prepared her resume and sent it to the school. Then she was called for an interview. She impressed the interviewers so much that she got the job. Here is the resume she prepared.

Name: Pegah Abassi

Address: 301-8 Park Place, Montreal, Quebec

Postal Code: H3N 5H5

Telephone: (514) 222-6262

▶ **CAREER GOALS**
Teach at the high school level
Get a masters degree in education

▶ **EDUCATION**
Cegep diploma, Dawson College*
B.Ed., McGill University

▶ **EMPLOYMENT HISTORY**

Describe two positions; the most recent first. Include volunteer and work experience.

Year(s): 2001–2005
Title or position: Lifeguard
Company/Organization: Lake Edwards Summer Camp
Duties: Supervised all the lifeguards on staff. Taught swimming.

Year(s): 2003–2004
Title or position: Part-time teacher
Company/Organization: Louis Papineau College
Duties: Taught English as a Second Language. Was responsible for extracurricular computer classes.

Very brief 1 or 2 line summary

▶ **SKILLS**
Communicate well in speaking and writing
Trilingual (English, French, Arabic)
High level of computer literacy

▶ **PERSONAL QUALITIES**
Dynamic, hard-working, and patient with adolescents

▶ **INTERESTS**
Reading, travelling, participating in triathlons (running, swimming and biking)

▶ **REFERENCES**

Someone who knows you very well

Name of Reference: Mr. Peter Lawrence
Title or Position: Director
Company/Organization: Lake Edwards Summer Camp
Work and/or Home Number: (450) 345-6789

Name of Reference: Mrs. Stella Dupont
Title or Position: Assistant Principal
Company/Organization: Louis Papineau College
Work and/or Home Number: (450) 997-6543

---

* Includes grades 12 and 13.

 Writing a Resume

STEP 4 PREPARE FOR THE ROLE OF JOB INTERVIEWER.

➤ Read the job advertisement of another group.

> EXAMPLE: Group A1 reads advertisement A2.
> Group A2 reads advertisement A1.

➤ To help you understand the vocabulary in the new job ad, review the vocabulary activity in your workbook.

> EXAMPLE: Group A1 reviews the vocabulary activity for advertisement A2.

 page 100 Do WB 1. Vocabulary in Job Ads

Group A		Group B		Group C		Group D	
A1	A2	B1	B2	C1	C2	D1	D2
Read ad A2.	Read ad A1.	Read ad B2.	Read ad B1.	Read ad C2.	Read ad C1.	Read ad D2.	Read ad D1.

STEP 5 WRITE INTERVIEW QUESTIONS FOR THE INTERVIEWER.

➤ In your group, prepare a list of questions to ask when you interview the job candidates.

> EXAMPLE: Group A1 decides what questions they'll ask Group A2 about the librarian's job.

➤ Decide what questions each group member will ask.

➤ Use Reading 3: Interviewer's Notes to help you.

➤ Make a list of qualities needed by the successful candidate for the job ad.

> EXAMPLE: *We need someone who is patient.*

➤ Review your interview questions. Take time to practise them. Ask your teacher to listen.

 page 104 Do WB 3. Interview Worksheet

 Answering Questions in an Interview

Feel Empowered

Before you go to a job interview, practise answering the questions out loud with a friend.

Interview Notes

READING 3

➤ Read the questions that one interviewer asked Pegah in an interview.

➤ Use them to help you with your interview questions.

	Candidate 1 Name: Pegah Abassi
• Where did you take your teacher training? • How much experience do you have with young people?	Studied at McGill University in the teacher-training program. Has some experience with young people.
• What are your personal qualities?	Dynamic and hard-working.
• What are your skills?	Communicates well and has a high level of computer literacy.
• Where have you worked before?	Taught part-time in a private high school. Did some extracurricular work after school. Summer camp and substitute teaching.
• What areas do you need to work on?	Needs to work on her discipline skills with young people.

STEP 6 LISTEN TO A JOB COUNSELLOR.

➤ Before beginning the job interviews, listen to a conversation between a job applicant and a job counsellor.

Advice for a Job Interview

LISTENING
WRITING

➤ Listen to some advice to help you play the roles of job applicant and counsellor.

➤ While listening, take notes. What advice does the counsellor give Pegah?

EXAMPLE: *Show that you are motivated and enthusiastic*

 page 104 Do WB 4. Listening for Details

 Talking About Job Duties

STEP 7 INTERVIEW THE JOB CANDIDATES.

➤ Now begin the job interviews. Your teacher and the rest of the class will listen to each interview.

> EXAMPLE: Group A1 interviews the applicants in Group A2.
> Then Group A2 will interview the applicants in Group A1.

➤ Follow what each applicant says using the interview checklist in your workbook.

➤ In your group, decide on the best person for the position.

Group A		Group B		Group C		Group D	
A1	A2	B1	B2	C1	C2	D1	D2
Interviewers	Job applicants	Interviewers	Job applicants	Interviewers	Job applicants	Interviewers	Job applicants

 page 105 Do WB 5. Interview Checklist

STEP 8 SWITCH ROLES AND CONTINUE THE INTERVIEWS.

➤ Change roles.

> EXAMPLE: Interviewers in A2 interview the job applicants in A1, each in turn.

➤ Follow what each applicant says using the interview checklist in your workbook.

➤ In your group, decide on the best person for the position.

 page 105 Do WB 5. Interview Checklist

Group A		Group B		Group C		Group D	
A1	A2	B1	B2	C1	C2	D1	D2
Job applicants	Interviewers	Job applicants	Interviewers	Job applicants	Interviewers	Job applicants	Interviewers

STEP 9 WRITE A MEMO TO THE EMPLOYER.

Memo to Employer

READING 4
WRITING

➤ Read this memo to an employer recommending an applicant for a position.

TO:	**Principal**	DATE:	**May 20, 2005**
FROM:	**Freda Horowitz, Head of Selection Committee**	SUBJECT:	**Hiring of new teacher**

We would like to recommend Ms. Abassi for the position of teacher at your school. We were most impressed with the professionalism she showed during the interview. Ms. Abassi has strong personal qualities. She is motivated and enthusiastic. She also possesses the following professional skills: good computer and teaching skills.

We think that she will make an excellent addition to your school because she has many good qualities as a teacher. Enclosed is a copy of our report.

FH

➤ Work with your group and prepare a memo giving your reasons for choosing the best candidate. Use the model above to write the memo.

> EXAMPLE: Interviewers in Group A1 recommend the best job applicant in Group A2.

➤ Use the information from the interview checklist that you filled in.

➤ Choose a member from your subgroup to report to the whole class.

➤ Say which of the applicants gets the job and for what reasons.

 page 106 Do WB 6. Memo to an Employer

STEP 10 CHECK YOUR PROGRESS.

➤ Discuss the role-play activity with your group.

➤ Assess your performance as an interviewer and as a job applicant.

➤ Think about how well you participated in all the activities. Think about what you need to work on.

 page 107 Do WB 7. How Well Did I Do?